Buffy
THE HIGH SCHOOL YEARS™

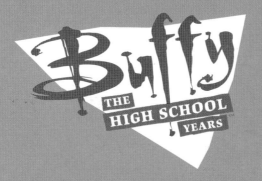

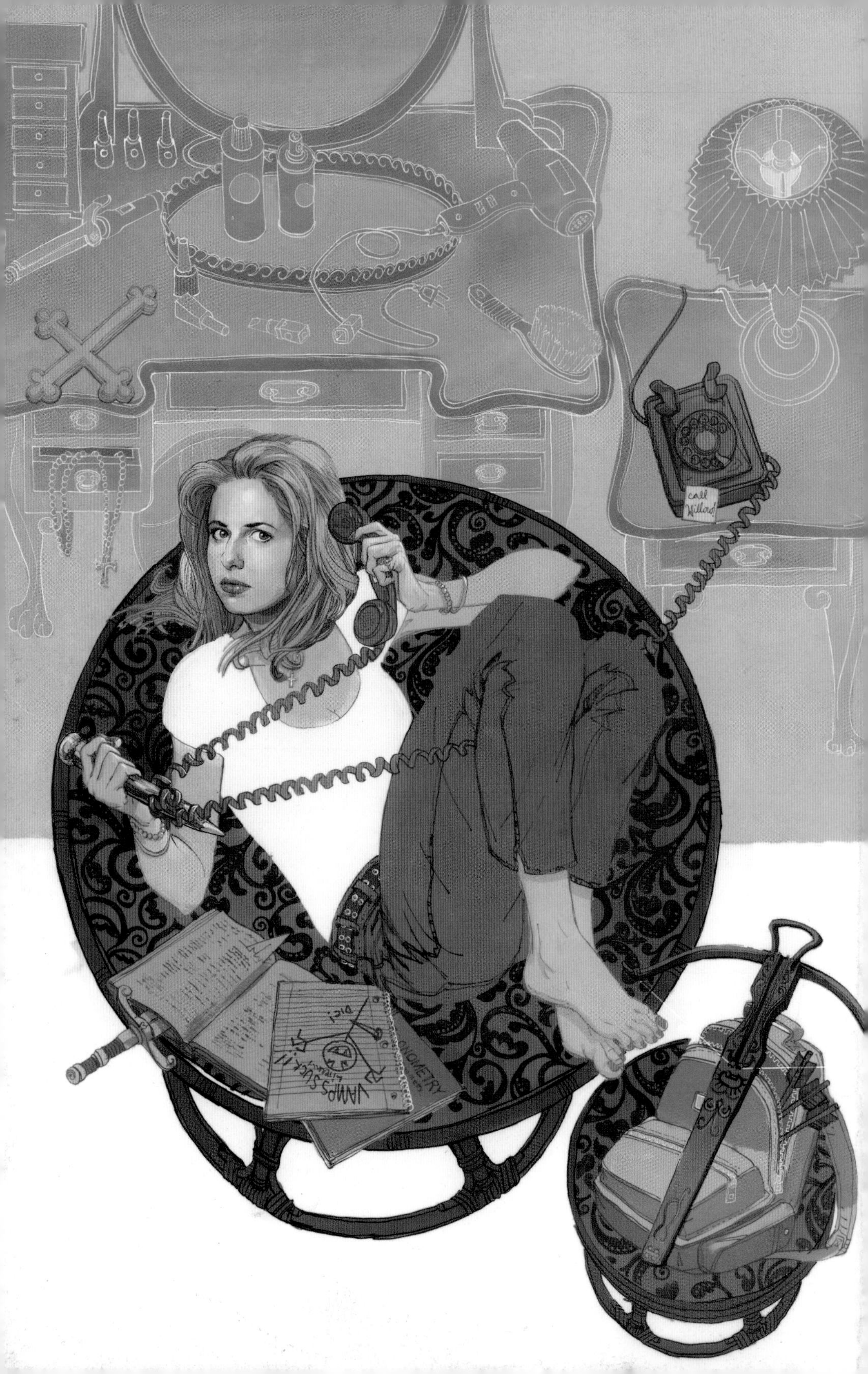
call Willow!
DIE!
VAMPS SUCK!!
Literally
GONOMETRY

Buffy

THE HIGH SCHOOL YEARS

FREAKS & GEEKS

SCRIPT
FAITH ERIN HICKS

ART
YISHAN LI

COLORS **ROD ESPINOSA**
WITH ASSISTANCE FROM **TONY GALVAN**

LETTERING
RICHARD STARKINGS & COMICRAFT'S
JIMMY BETANCOURT

COVER ART **SCOTT FISCHER**

EXECUTIVE PRODUCER **JOSS WHEDON**

DARK HORSE BOOKS

President & Publisher
MIKE RICHARDSON

Editors
FREDDYE MILLER & SIERRA HAHN

Designer
JUSTIN COUCH

Digital Art Technician
CHRISTIANNE GOUDREAU

Special thanks to Nicole Spiegel and Josh Izzo at Twentieth Century Fox,
Daniel Kaminsky, and Becca J. Sadowsky.

This story takes place during *Buffy the Vampire Slayer* Season 1, created by Joss Whedon.

First edition: June 2016 | ISBN 978-1-61655-667-9 | 10 9 8 7 6 5 4 3 2 1

Published by Dark Horse Books, a division of Dark Horse Comics, Inc.
10956 SE Main Street, Milwaukie, OR 97222 | DarkHorse.com

Neil Hankerson Executive Vice President · Tom Weddle Chief Financial Officer · Randy Stradley Vice
President of Publishing · Michael Martens Vice President of Book Trade Sales · Matt Parkinson Vice
President of Marketing · David Scroggy Vice President of Product Development · Dale LaFountain
Vice President of Information Technology · Cara Niece Vice President of Production and Scheduling
· Nick McWhorter Vice President of Media Licensing · Ken Lizzi General Counsel · Dave Marshall
Editor in Chief · Davey Estrada Editorial Director · Scott Allie Executive Senior Editor · Chris Warner
Senior Books Editor · Cary Grazzini Director of Print and Development · Lia Ribacchi Art Director ·
Mark Bernardi Director of Digital Publishing · Michael Gombos Director of International Publishing
and Licensing

To find a comics shop in your area, call the Comic Shop Locator Service toll-free at (888) 266-4226.
International Licensing: 503-905-2377

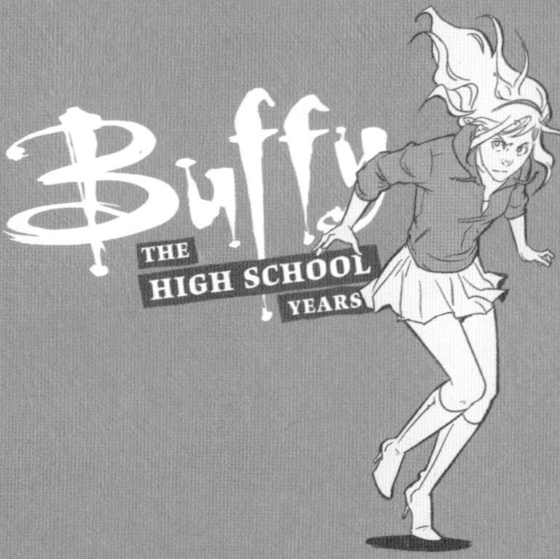
Buffy
THE
HIGH SCHOOL
YEARS

[redacted]

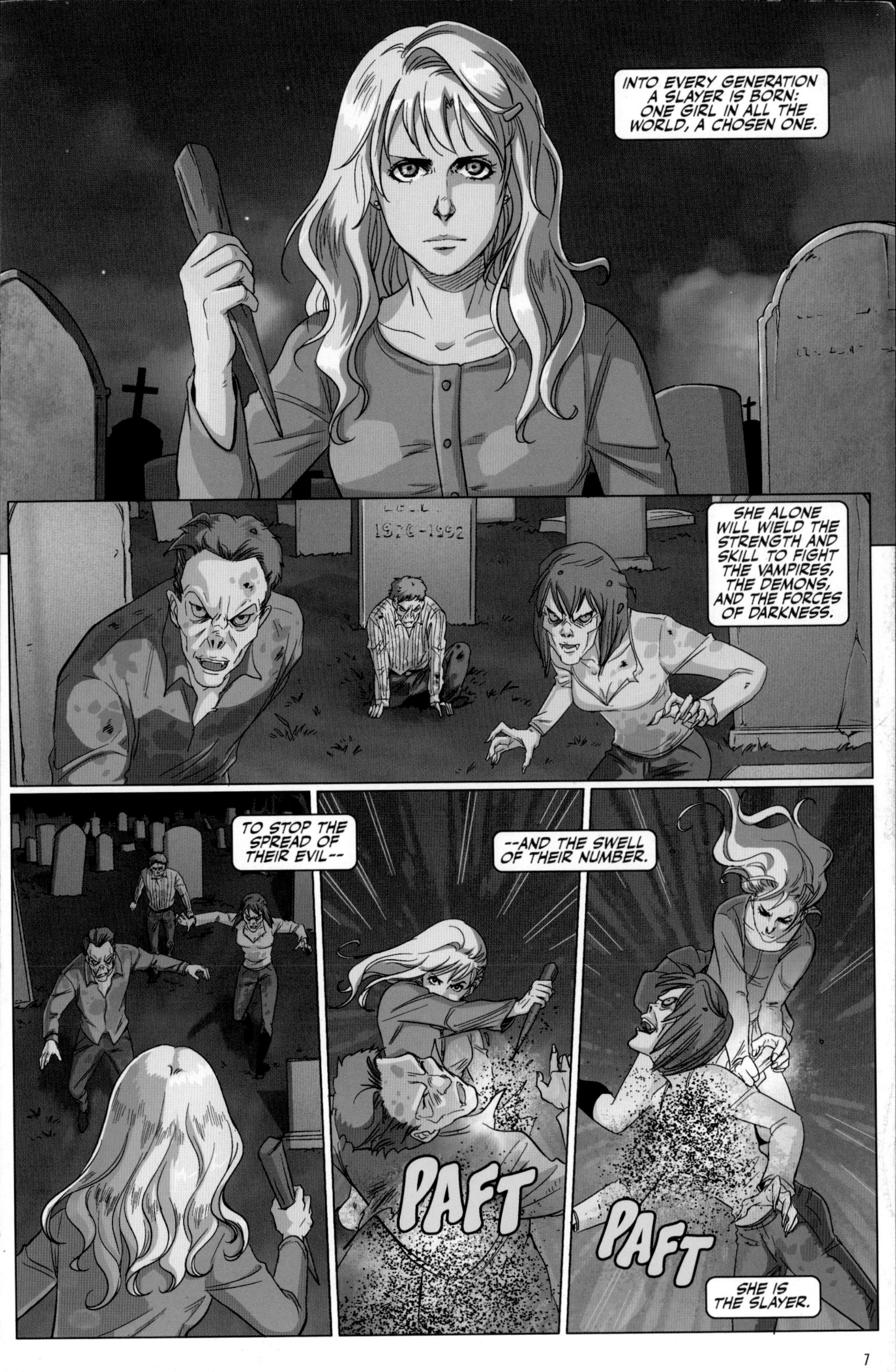
INTO EVERY GENERATION A SLAYER IS BORN: ONE GIRL IN ALL THE WORLD, A CHOSEN ONE.
1976-1992
SHE ALONE WILL WIELD THE STRENGTH AND SKILL TO FIGHT THE VAMPIRES, THE DEMONS, AND THE FORCES OF DARKNESS.
TO STOP THE SPREAD OF THEIR EVIL--
--AND THE SWELL OF THEIR NUMBER.
PAFT
PAFT
SHE IS THE SLAYER.

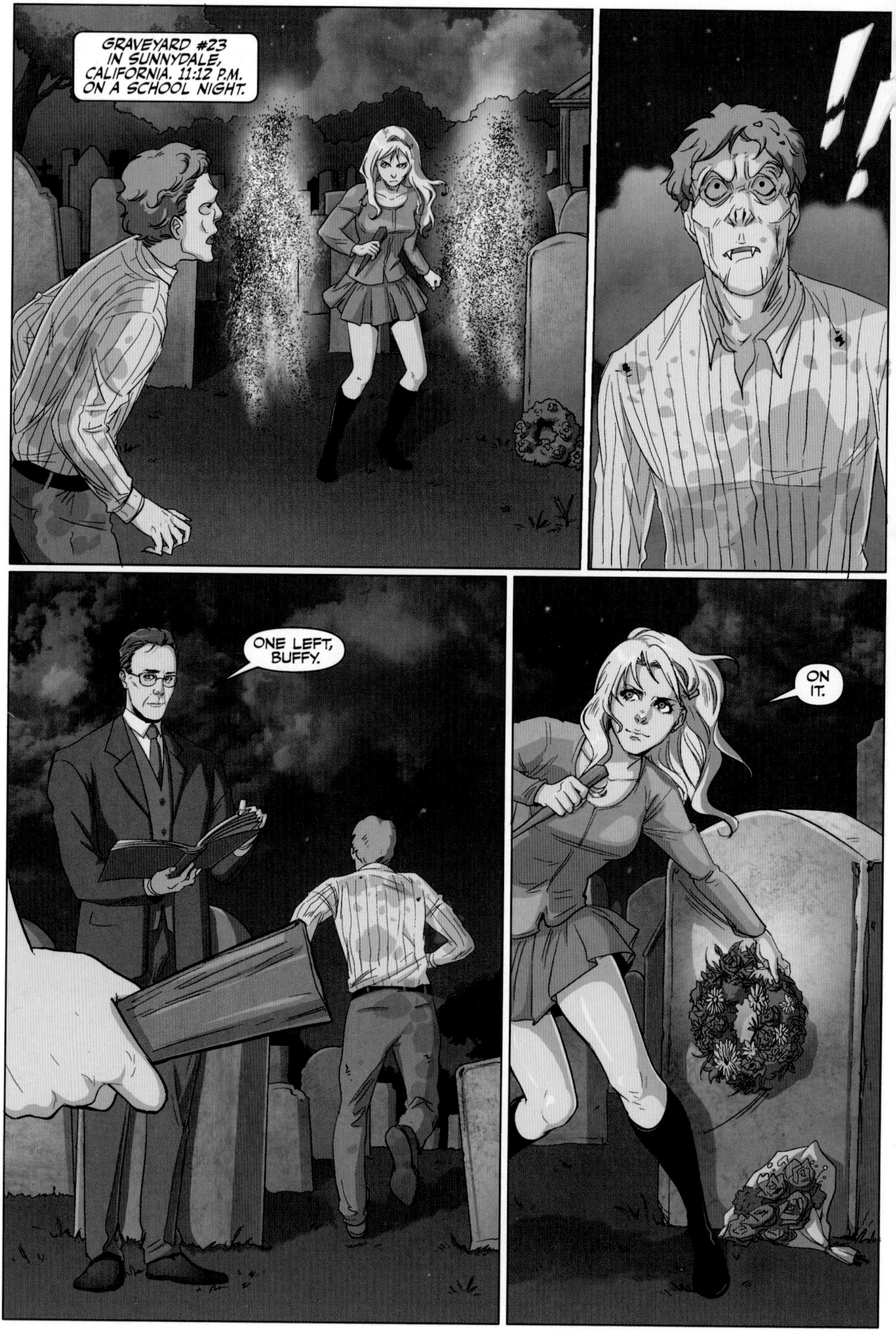
GRAVEYARD #23 IN SUNNYDALE, CALIFORNIA. 11:12 P.M. ON A SCHOOL NIGHT.
!!
ONE LEFT, BUFFY.
ON IT.

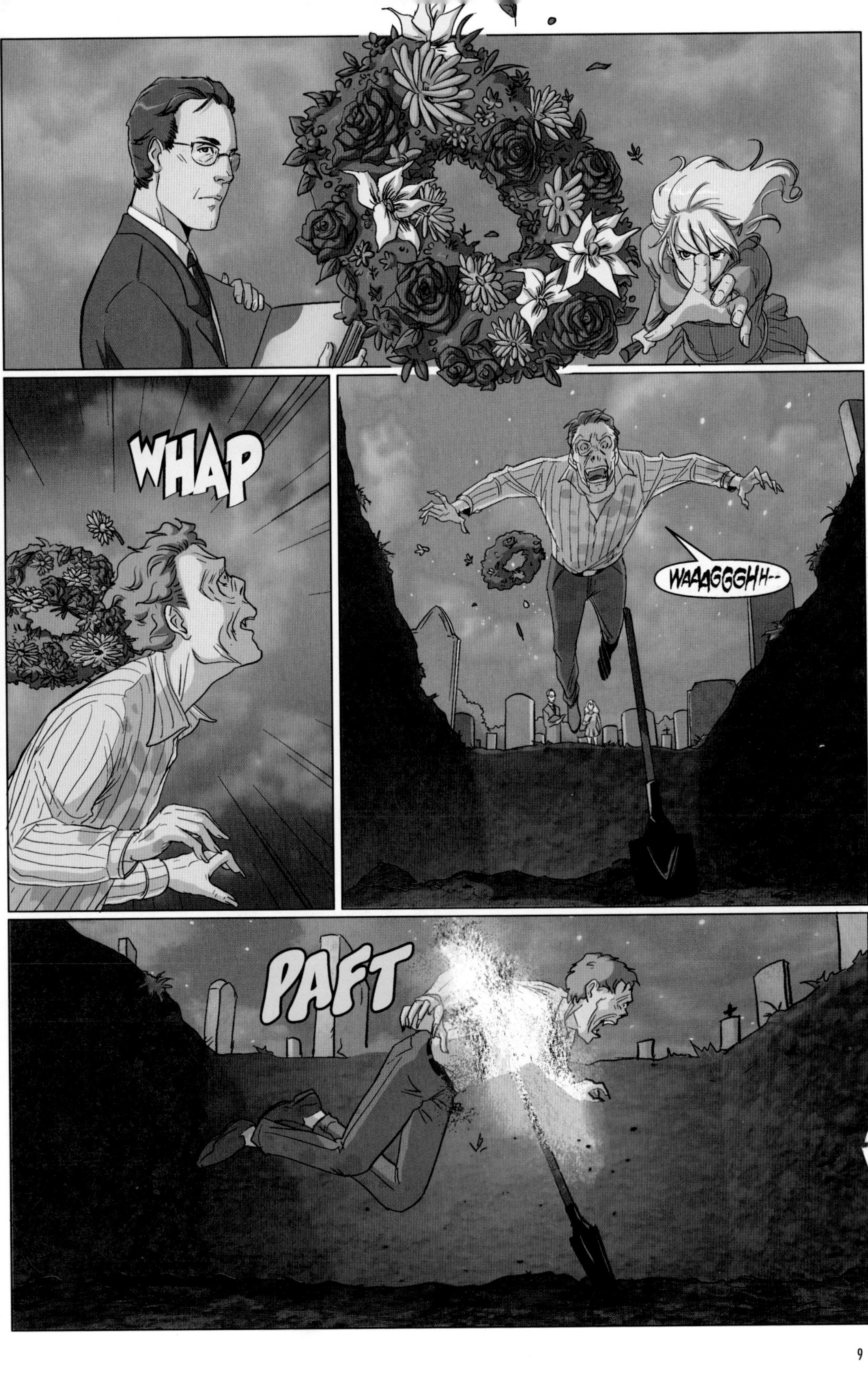
WHAP
WAAAGGGHH--
PAFT

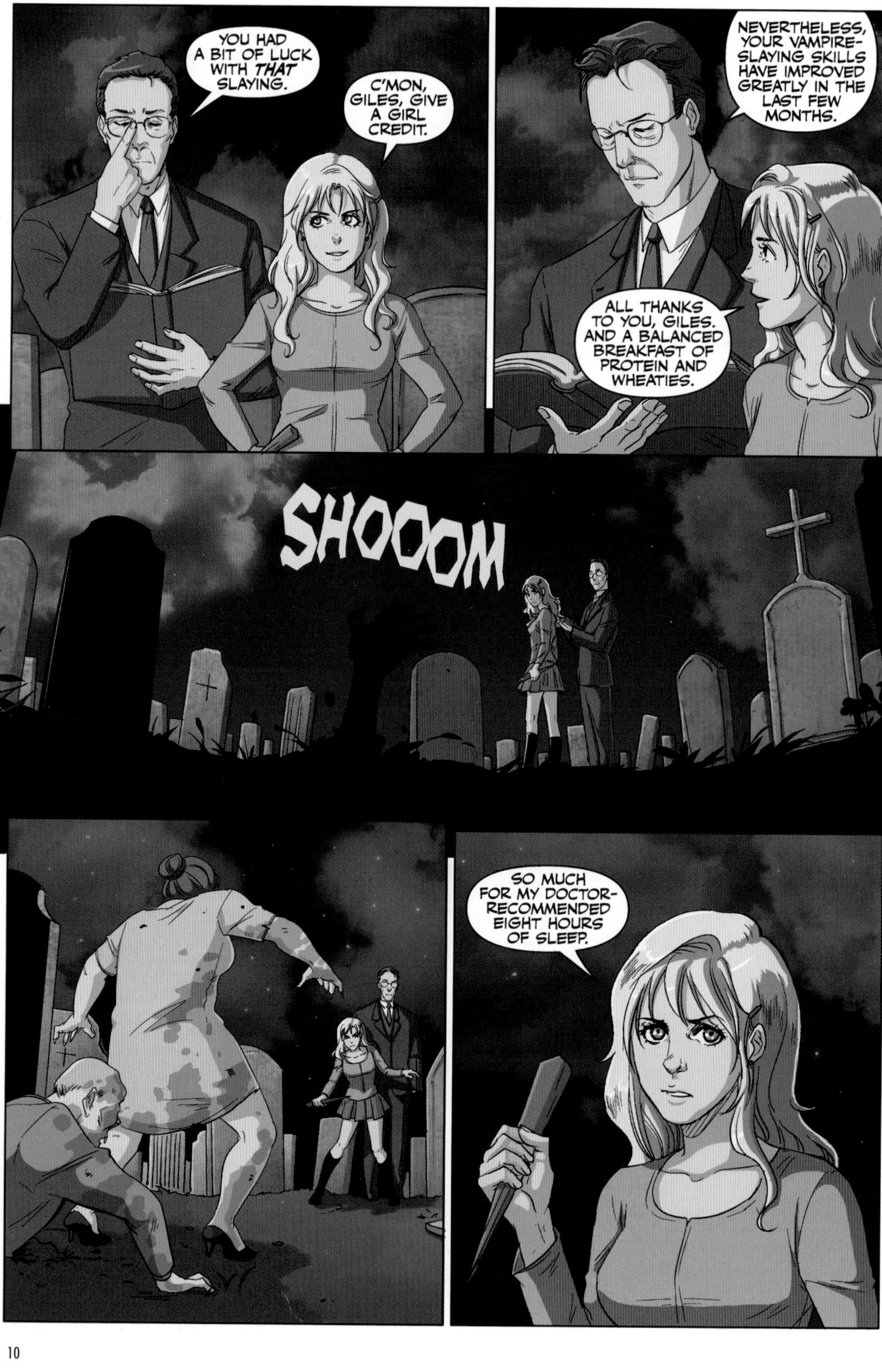
YOU HAD A BIT OF LUCK WITH *THAT* SLAYING.
C'MON, GILES, GIVE A GIRL CREDIT.
NEVERTHELESS, YOUR VAMPIRE-SLAYING SKILLS HAVE IMPROVED GREATLY IN THE LAST FEW MONTHS.
ALL THANKS TO YOU, GILES. AND A BALANCED BREAKFAST OF PROTEIN AND WHEATIES.
SHOOOM
SO MUCH FOR MY DOCTOR-RECOMMENDED EIGHT HOURS OF SLEEP.

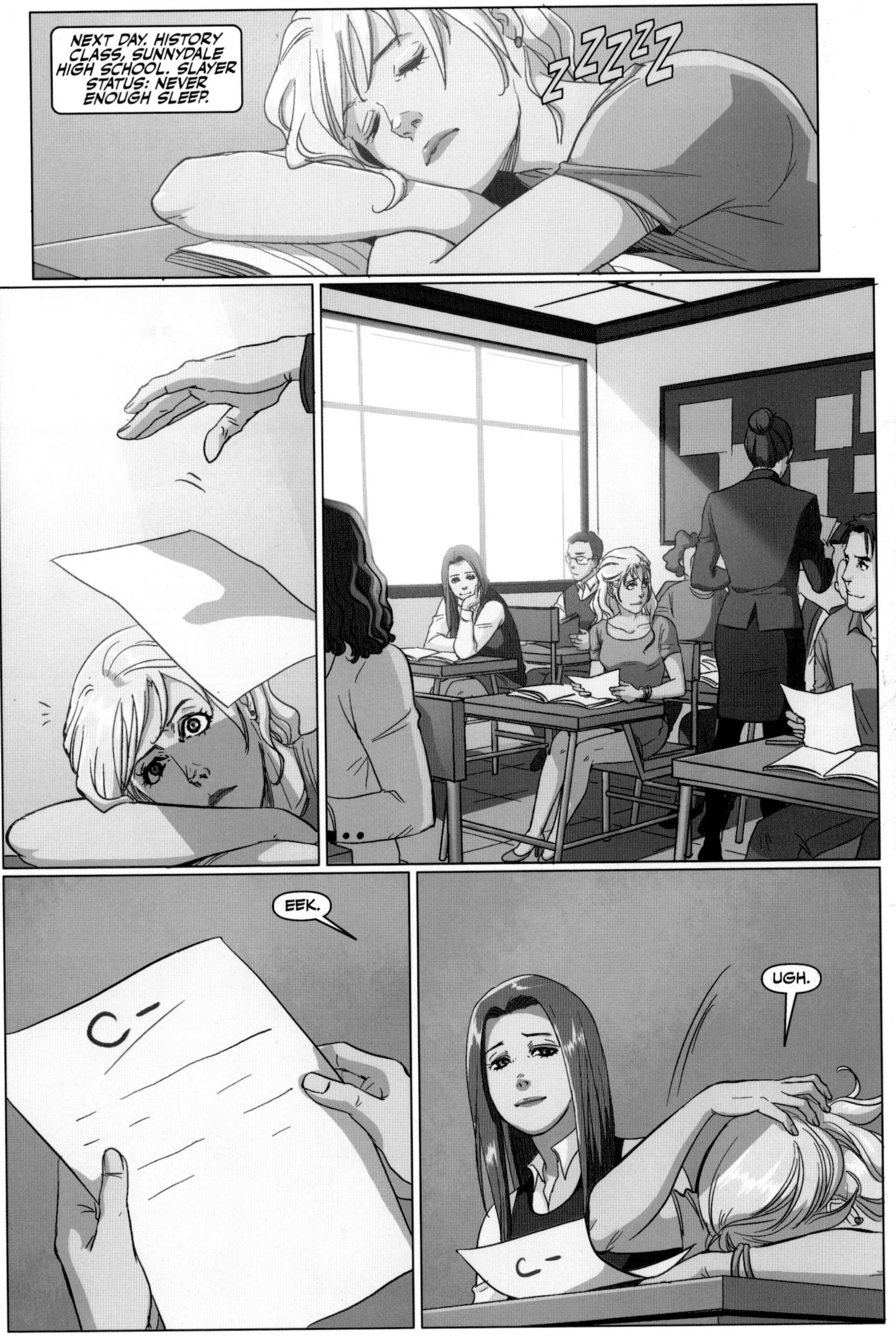
NEXT DAY. HISTORY CLASS, SUNNYDALE HIGH SCHOOL. SLAYER STATUS: NEVER ENOUGH SLEEP.
ZZZZZ
EEK.
C-
UGH.
C-

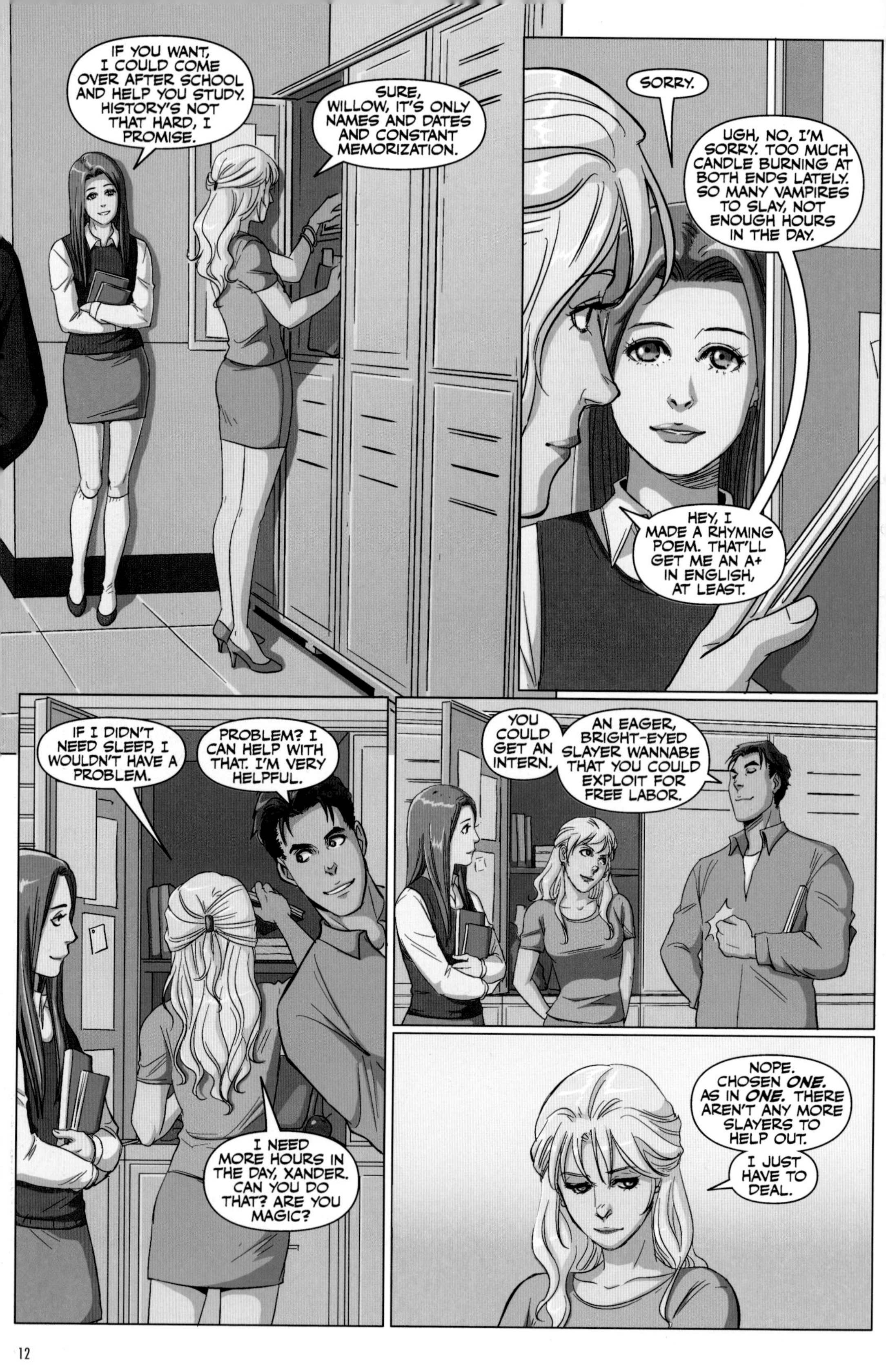
IF YOU WANT, I COULD COME OVER AFTER SCHOOL AND HELP YOU STUDY. HISTORY'S NOT THAT HARD, I PROMISE.
SURE, WILLOW, IT'S ONLY NAMES AND DATES AND CONSTANT MEMORIZATION.
SORRY.
UGH, NO, I'M SORRY. TOO MUCH CANDLE BURNING AT BOTH ENDS LATELY. SO MANY VAMPIRES TO SLAY, NOT ENOUGH HOURS IN THE DAY.
HEY, I MADE A RHYMING POEM. THAT'LL GET ME AN A+ IN ENGLISH, AT LEAST.
IF I DIDN'T NEED SLEEP, I WOULDN'T HAVE A PROBLEM.
PROBLEM? I CAN HELP WITH THAT. I'M VERY HELPFUL.
I NEED MORE HOURS IN THE DAY, XANDER. CAN YOU DO THAT? ARE YOU MAGIC?
YOU COULD GET AN INTERN.
AN EAGER, BRIGHT-EYED SLAYER WANNABE THAT YOU COULD EXPLOIT FOR FREE LABOR.
NOPE. CHOSEN *ONE.* AS IN *ONE.* THERE AREN'T ANY MORE SLAYERS TO HELP OUT.
I JUST HAVE TO DEAL.

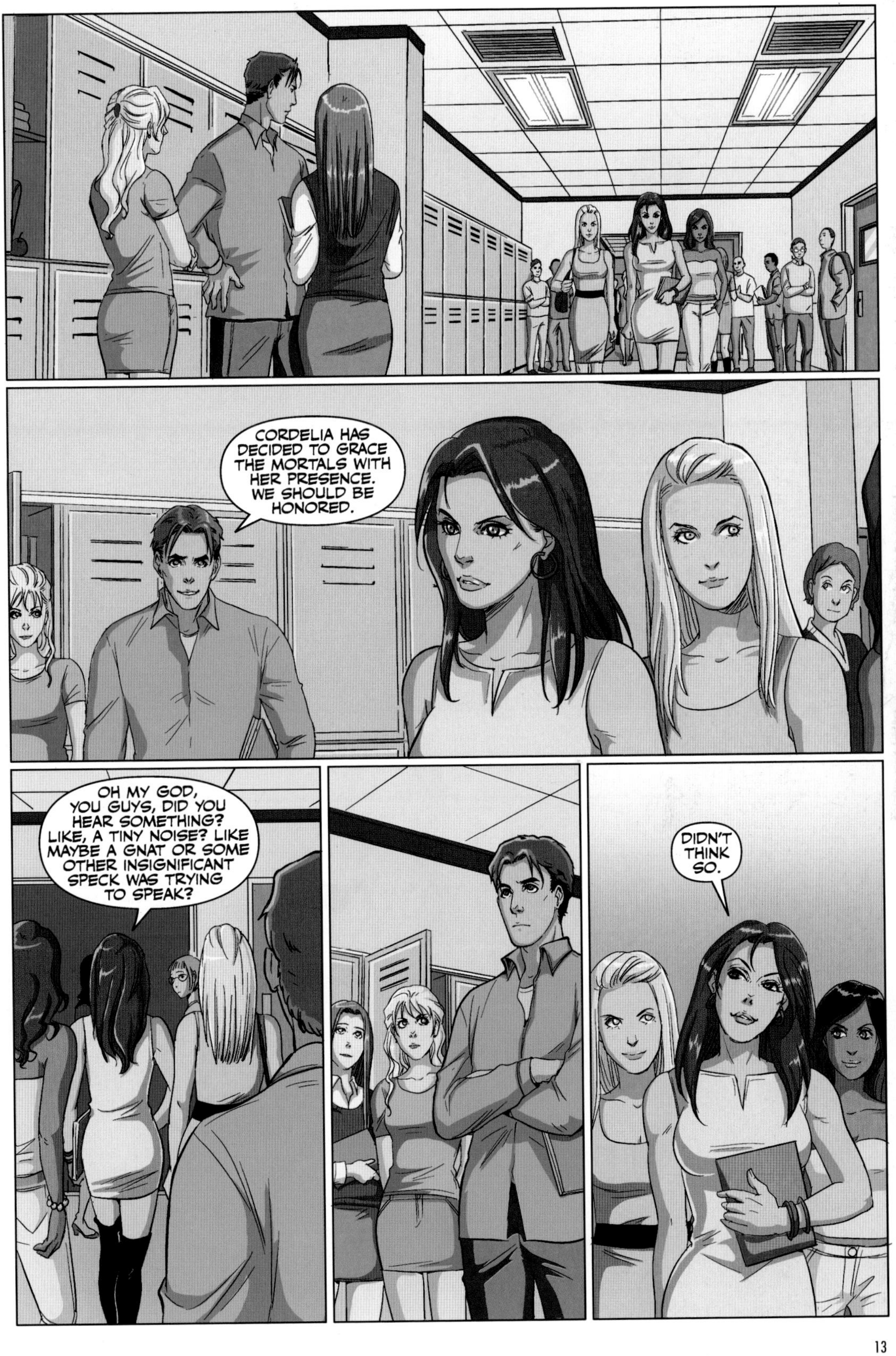
CORDELIA HAS DECIDED TO GRACE THE MORTALS WITH HER PRESENCE. WE SHOULD BE HONORED.
OH MY GOD, YOU GUYS, DID YOU HEAR SOMETHING? LIKE, A TINY NOISE? LIKE MAYBE A GNAT OR SOME OTHER INSIGNIFICANT SPECK WAS TRYING TO SPEAK?
DIDN'T THINK SO.

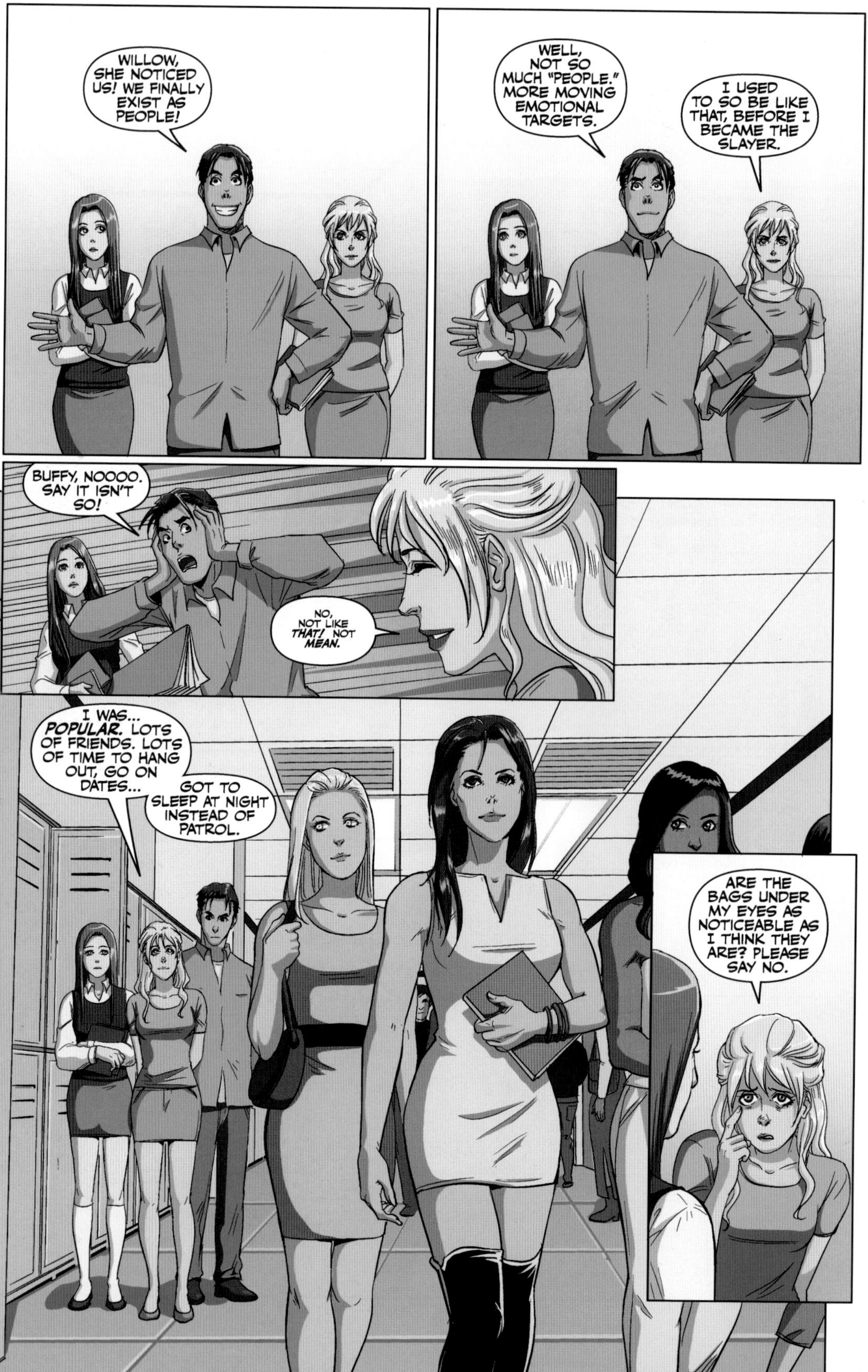
WILLOW, SHE NOTICED US! WE FINALLY EXIST AS PEOPLE!
WELL, NOT SO MUCH "PEOPLE." MORE MOVING EMOTIONAL TARGETS.
I USED TO SO BE LIKE THAT, BEFORE I BECAME THE SLAYER.
BUFFY, NOOOO. SAY IT ISN'T SO!
NO, NOT LIKE THAT! NOT MEAN.
I WAS... POPULAR. LOTS OF FRIENDS. LOTS OF TIME TO HANG OUT, GO ON DATES...
GOT TO SLEEP AT NIGHT INSTEAD OF PATROL.
ARE THE BAGS UNDER MY EYES AS NOTICEABLE AS I THINK THEY ARE? PLEASE SAY NO.

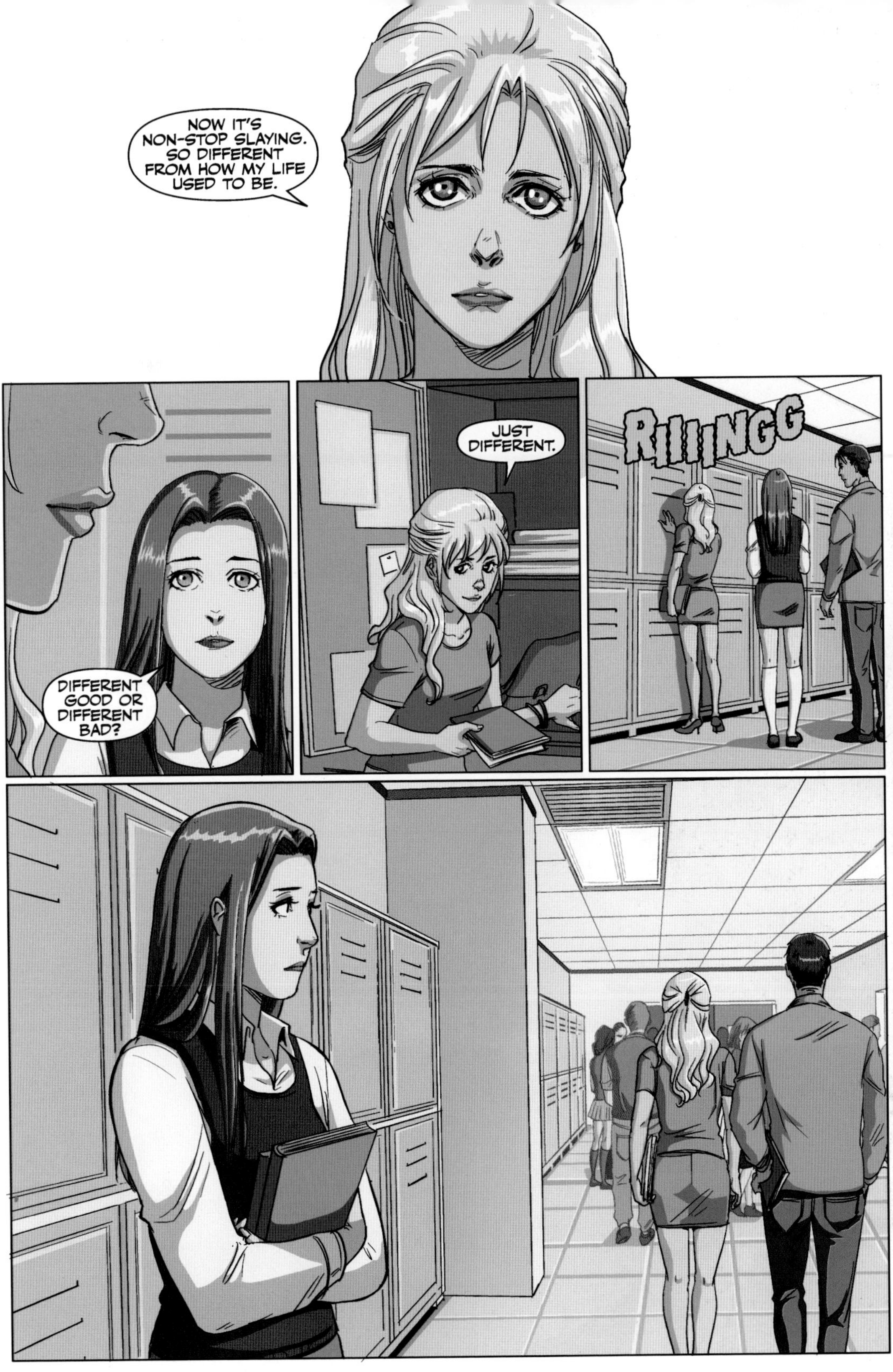
NOW IT'S NON-STOP SLAYING. SO DIFFERENT FROM HOW MY LIFE USED TO BE.
DIFFERENT GOOD OR DIFFERENT BAD?
JUST DIFFERENT.
RIIIINGG

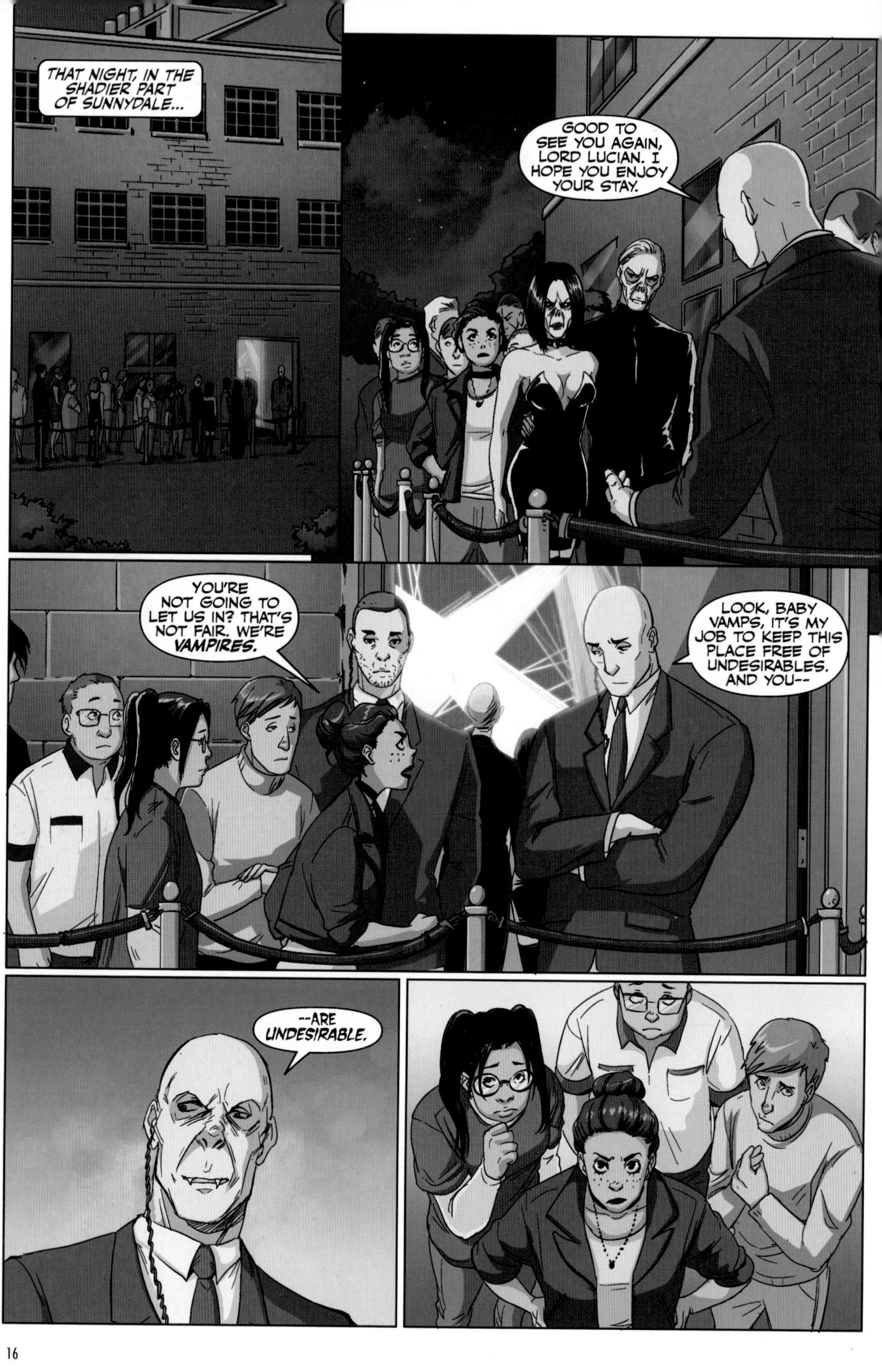
THAT NIGHT, IN THE SHADIER PART OF SUNNYDALE...
GOOD TO SEE YOU AGAIN, LORD LUCIAN. I HOPE YOU ENJOY YOUR STAY.
YOU'RE NOT GOING TO LET US IN? THAT'S NOT FAIR. WE'RE VAMPIRES.
LOOK, BABY VAMPS, IT'S MY JOB TO KEEP THIS PLACE FREE OF UNDESIRABLES. AND YOU--
--ARE UNDESIRABLE.

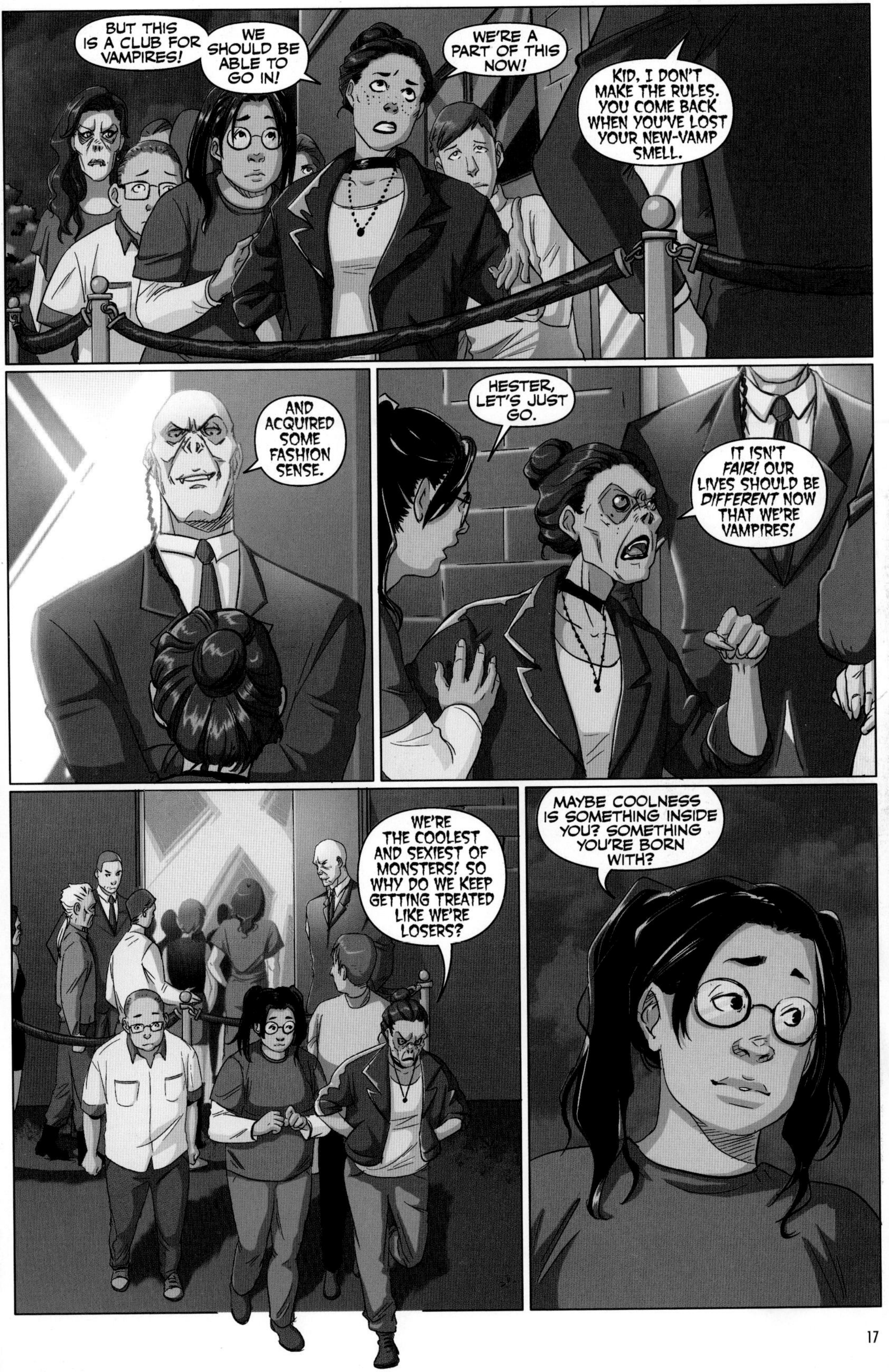
BUT THIS IS A CLUB FOR VAMPIRES!
WE SHOULD BE ABLE TO GO IN!
WE'RE A PART OF THIS NOW!
KID, I DON'T MAKE THE RULES. YOU COME BACK WHEN YOU'VE LOST YOUR NEW-VAMP SMELL.
AND ACQUIRED SOME FASHION SENSE.
HESTER, LET'S JUST GO.
IT ISN'T *FAIR!* OUR LIVES SHOULD BE *DIFFERENT* NOW THAT WE'RE VAMPIRES!
WE'RE THE COOLEST AND SEXIEST OF MONSTERS! SO WHY DO WE KEEP GETTING TREATED LIKE WE'RE LOSERS?
MAYBE COOLNESS IS SOMETHING INSIDE YOU? SOMETHING YOU'RE BORN WITH?

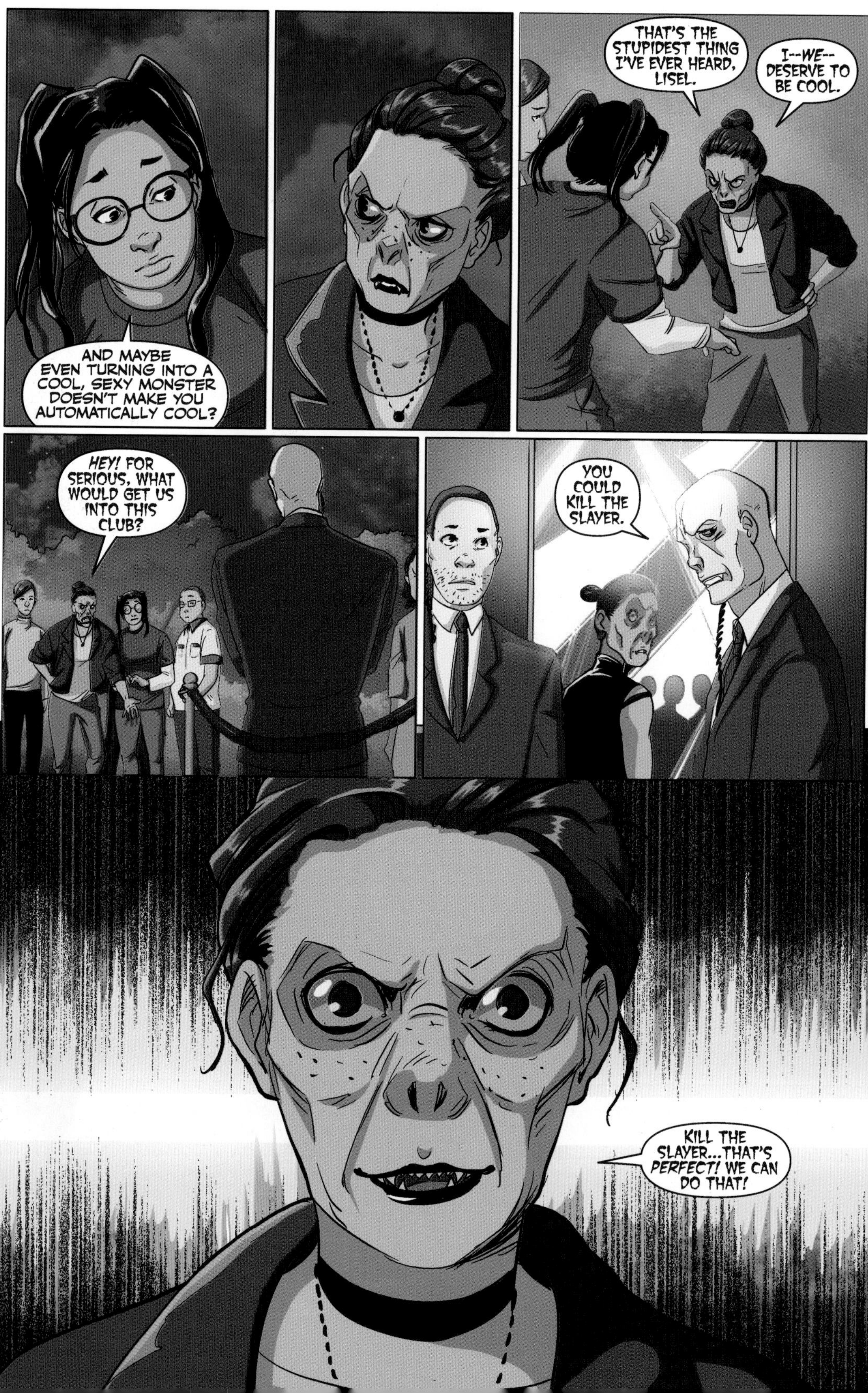
AND MAYBE EVEN TURNING INTO A COOL, SEXY MONSTER DOESN'T MAKE YOU AUTOMATICALLY COOL?
THAT'S THE STUPIDEST THING I'VE EVER HEARD, LISEL.
I--*WE*--DESERVE TO BE COOL.
HEY! FOR SERIOUS, WHAT WOULD GET US INTO THIS CLUB?
YOU COULD KILL THE SLAYER.
KILL THE SLAYER...THAT'S *PERFECT!* WE CAN DO THAT!

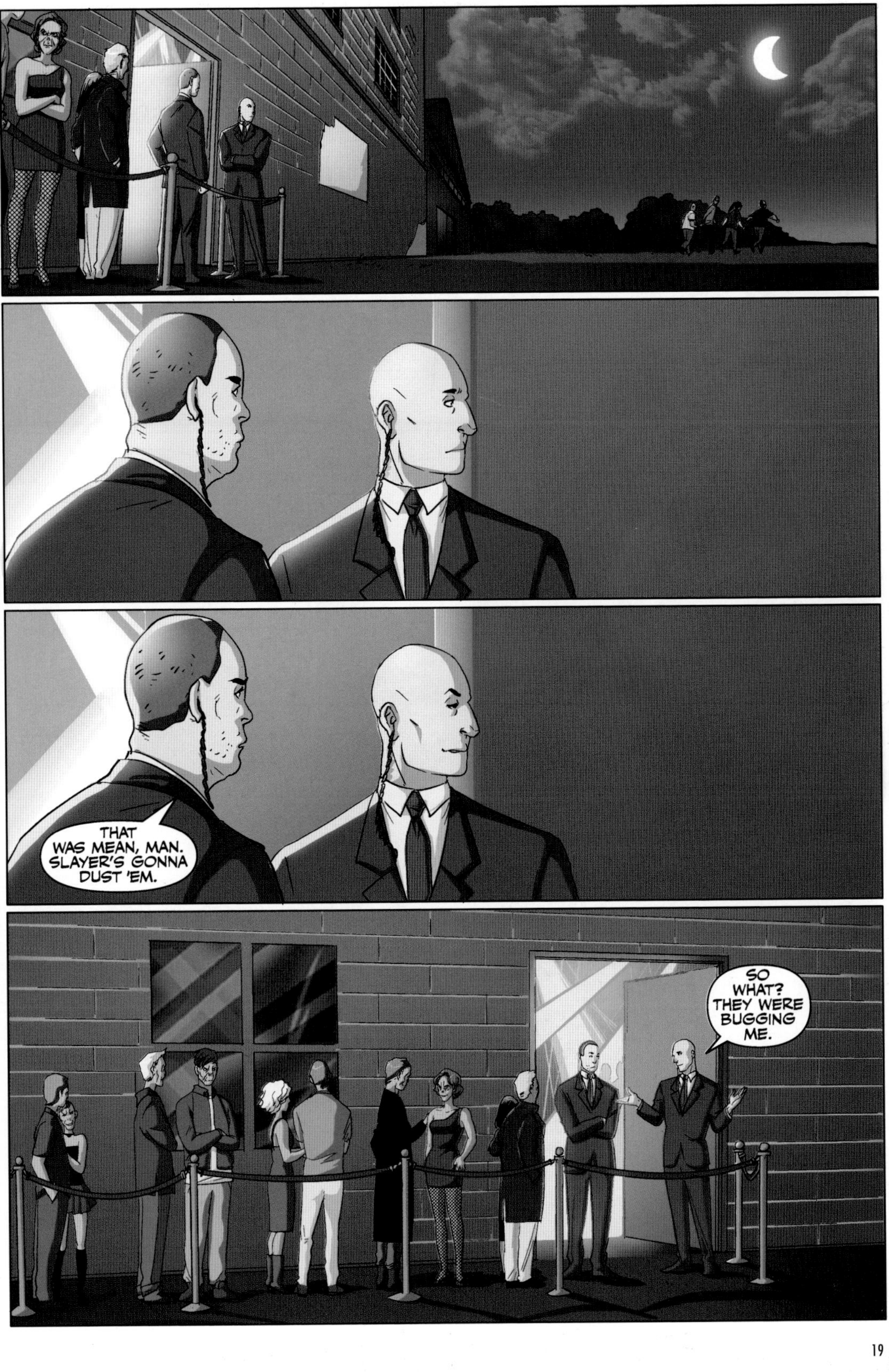
THAT WAS MEAN, MAN. SLAYER'S GONNA DUST 'EM.
SO WHAT? THEY WERE BUGGING ME.

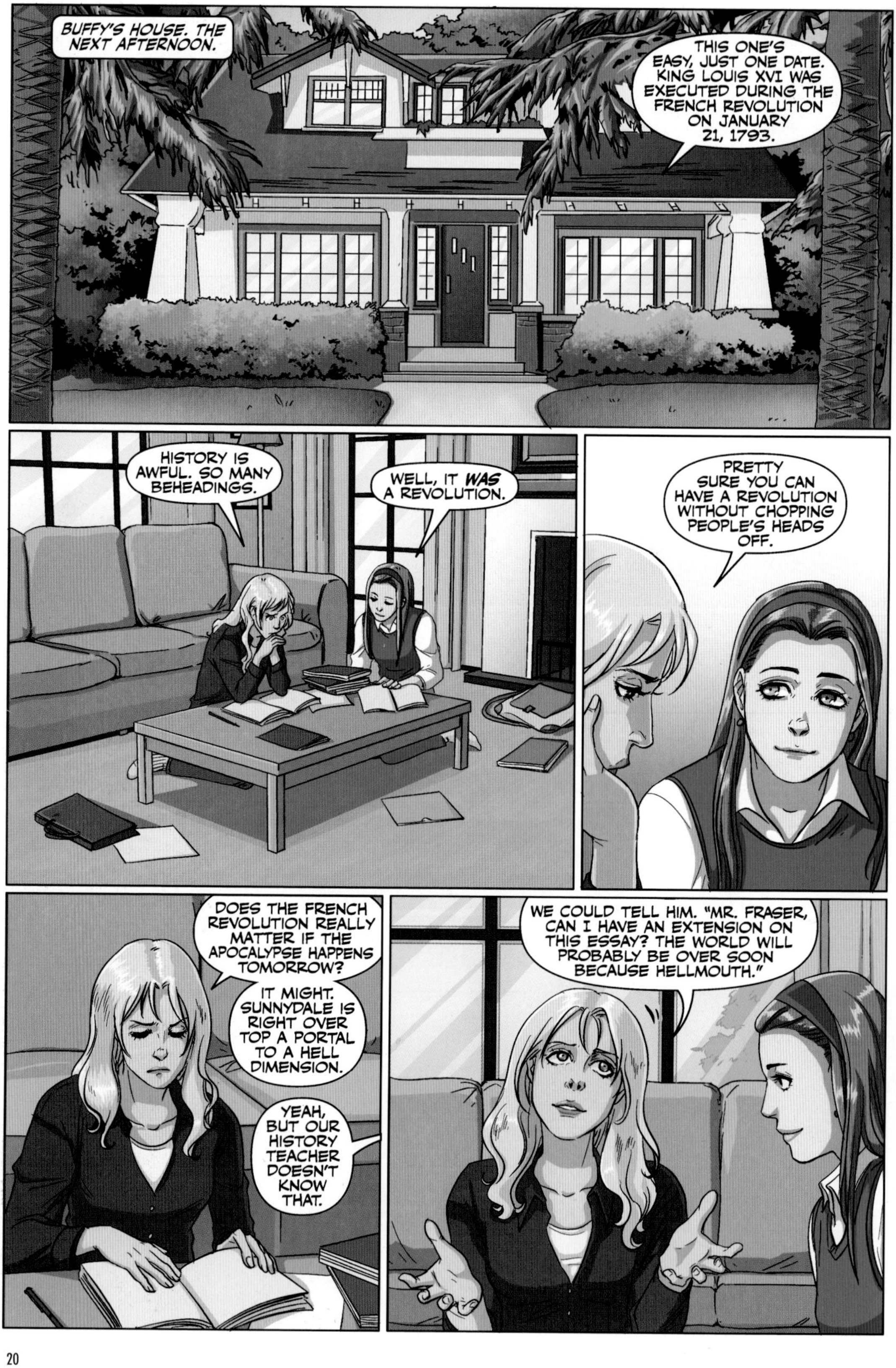
BUFFY'S HOUSE. THE NEXT AFTERNOON.
THIS ONE'S EASY, JUST ONE DATE. KING LOUIS XVI WAS EXECUTED DURING THE FRENCH REVOLUTION ON JANUARY 21, 1793.
HISTORY IS AWFUL. SO MANY BEHEADINGS.
WELL, IT *WAS* A REVOLUTION.
PRETTY SURE YOU CAN HAVE A REVOLUTION WITHOUT CHOPPING PEOPLE'S HEADS OFF.
DOES THE FRENCH REVOLUTION REALLY MATTER IF THE APOCALYPSE HAPPENS TOMORROW?
IT MIGHT. SUNNYDALE IS RIGHT OVER TOP A PORTAL TO A HELL DIMENSION.
YEAH, BUT OUR HISTORY TEACHER DOESN'T KNOW THAT.
WE COULD TELL HIM. "MR. FRASER, CAN I HAVE AN EXTENSION ON THIS ESSAY? THE WORLD WILL PROBABLY BE OVER SOON BECAUSE HELLMOUTH."

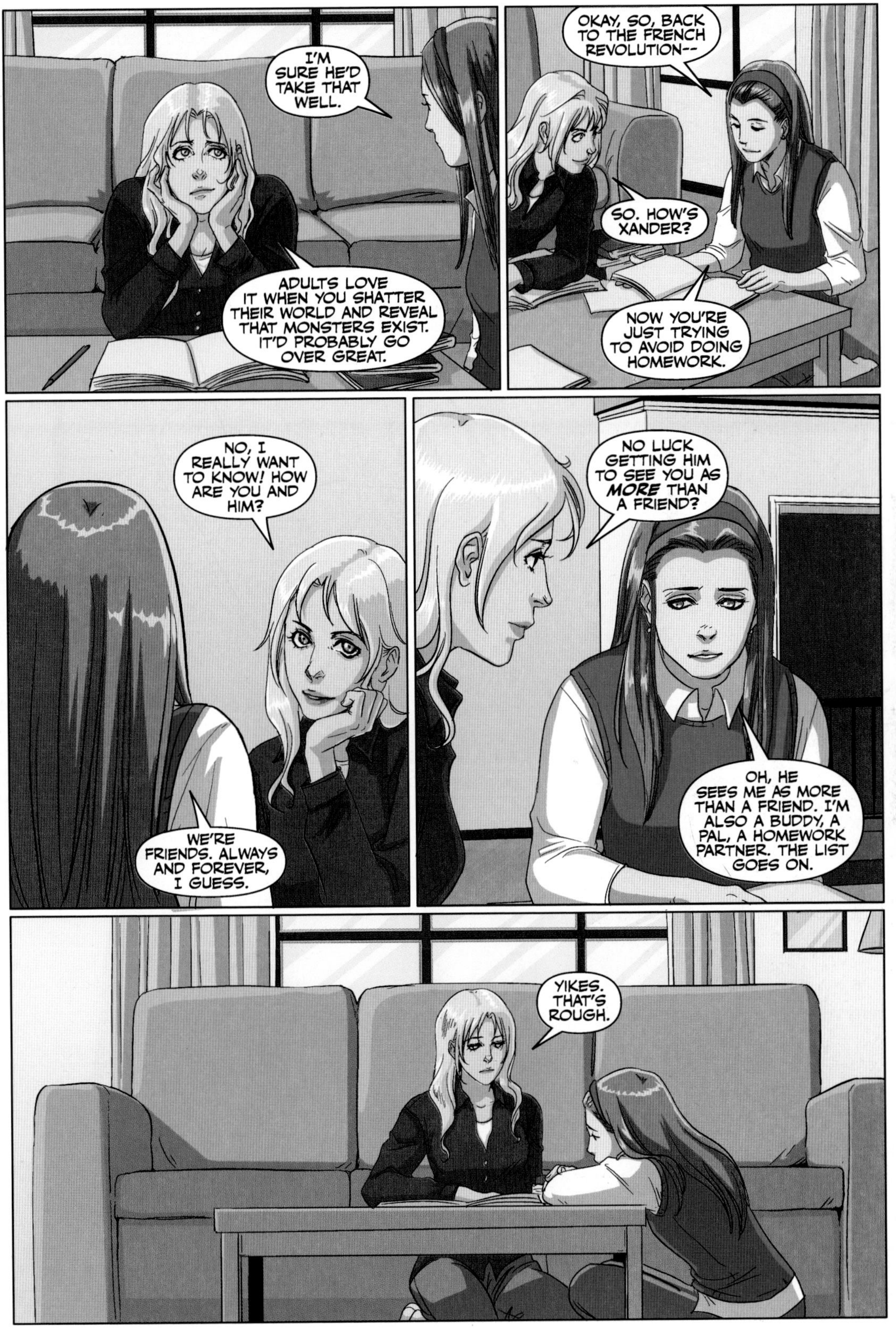

I'M SURE HE'D TAKE THAT WELL.
ADULTS LOVE IT WHEN YOU SHATTER THEIR WORLD AND REVEAL THAT MONSTERS EXIST. IT'D PROBABLY GO OVER GREAT.
OKAY, SO, BACK TO THE FRENCH REVOLUTION--
SO. HOW'S XANDER?
NOW YOU'RE JUST TRYING TO AVOID DOING HOMEWORK.
NO, I REALLY WANT TO KNOW! HOW ARE YOU AND HIM?
WE'RE FRIENDS. ALWAYS AND FOREVER, I GUESS.
NO LUCK GETTING HIM TO SEE YOU AS *MORE* THAN A FRIEND?
OH, HE SEES ME AS MORE THAN A FRIEND. I'M ALSO A BUDDY, A PAL, A HOMEWORK PARTNER. THE LIST GOES ON.
YIKES. THAT'S ROUGH.

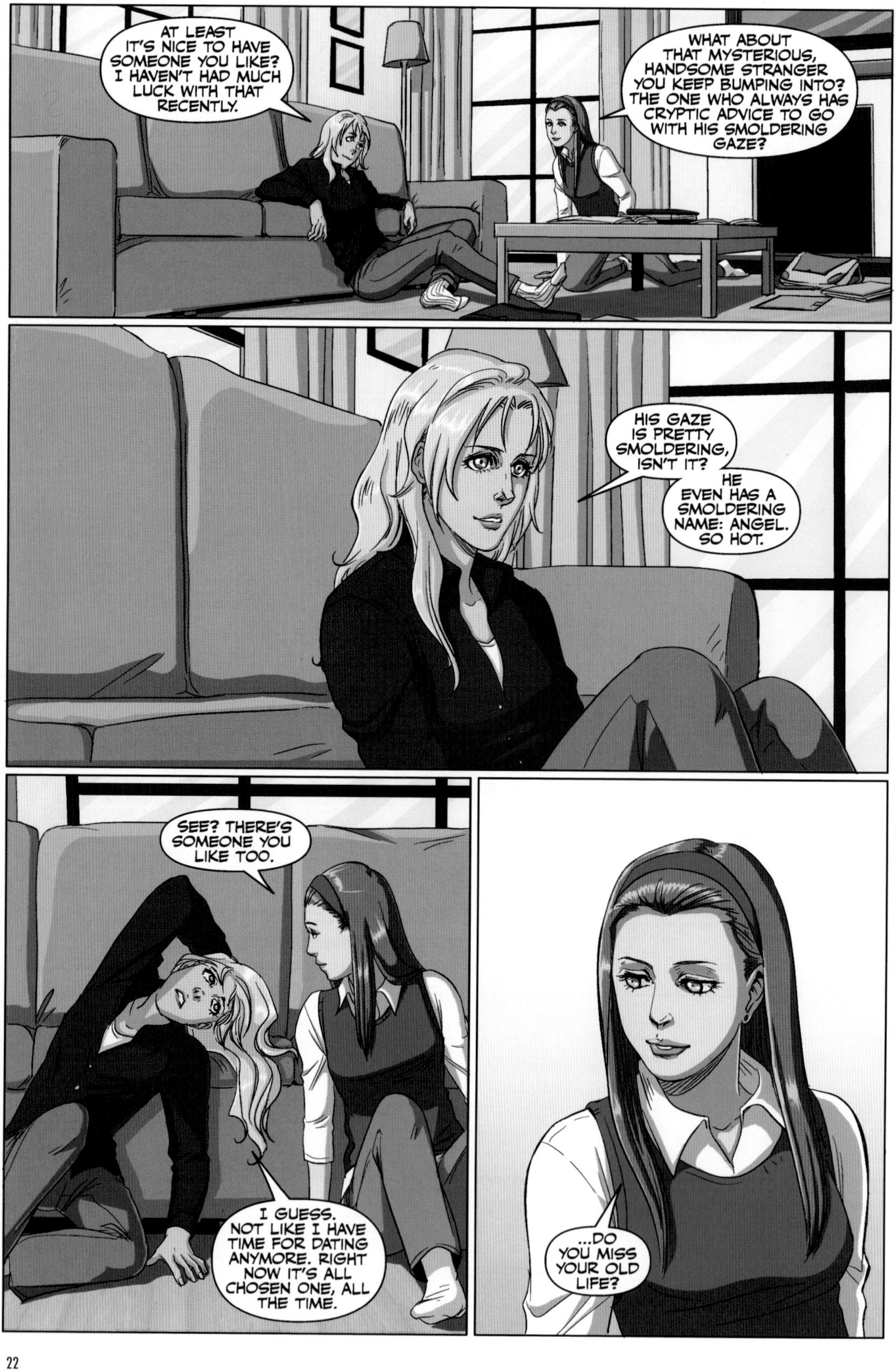
AT LEAST IT'S NICE TO HAVE SOMEONE YOU LIKE? I HAVEN'T HAD MUCH LUCK WITH THAT RECENTLY.
WHAT ABOUT THAT MYSTERIOUS, HANDSOME STRANGER YOU KEEP BUMPING INTO? THE ONE WHO ALWAYS HAS CRYPTIC ADVICE TO GO WITH HIS SMOLDERING GAZE?
HIS GAZE IS PRETTY SMOLDERING, ISN'T IT?
HE EVEN HAS A SMOLDERING NAME: ANGEL. SO HOT.
SEE? THERE'S SOMEONE YOU LIKE TOO.
I GUESS. NOT LIKE I HAVE TIME FOR DATING ANYMORE. RIGHT NOW IT'S ALL CHOSEN ONE, ALL THE TIME.
...DO YOU MISS YOUR OLD LIFE?

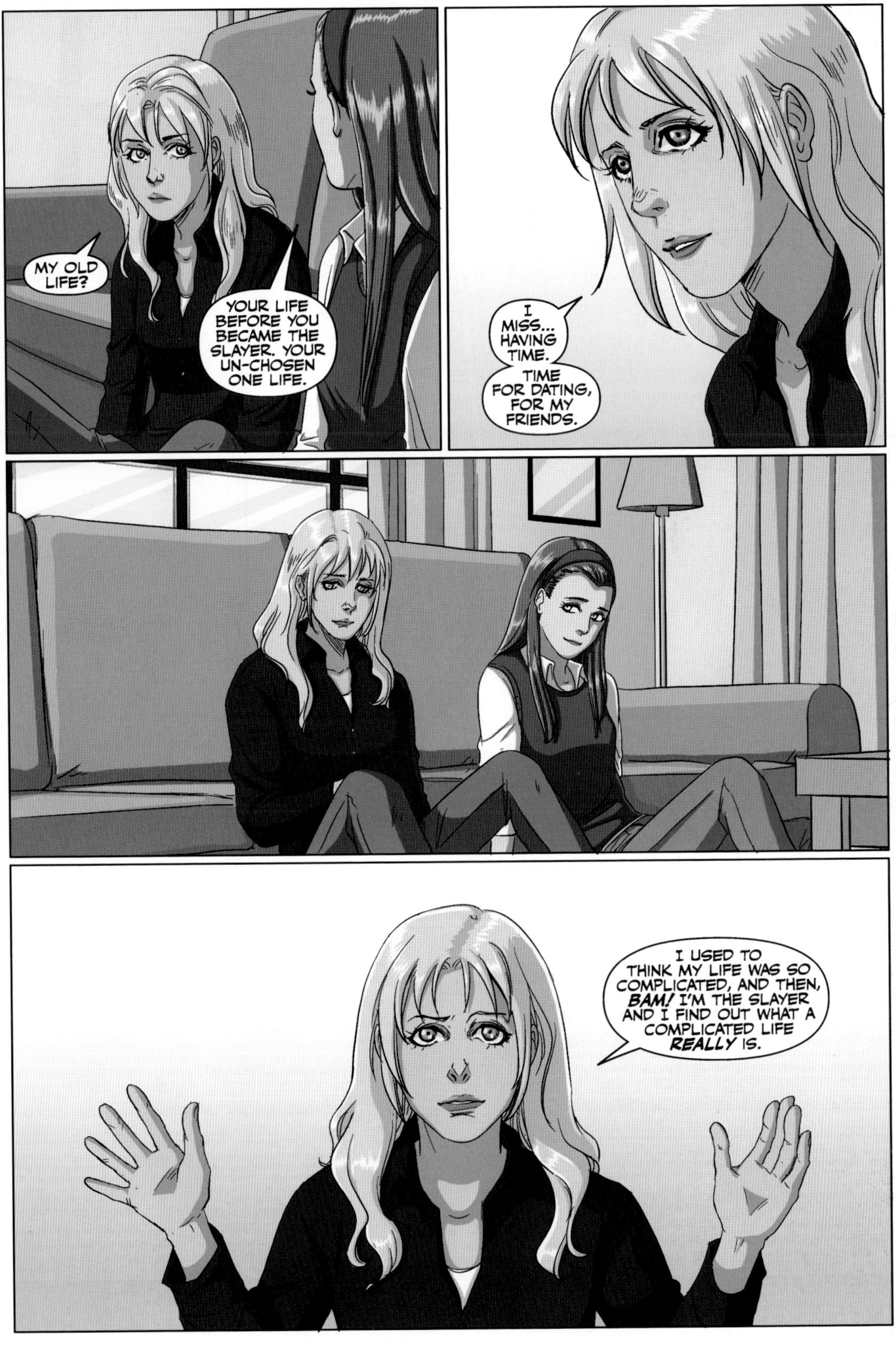
MY OLD LIFE?
YOUR LIFE BEFORE YOU BECAME THE SLAYER. YOUR UN-CHOSEN ONE LIFE.
I MISS... HAVING TIME.
TIME FOR DATING, FOR MY FRIENDS.
I USED TO THINK MY LIFE WAS SO COMPLICATED, AND THEN, BAM! I'M THE SLAYER AND I FIND OUT WHAT A COMPLICATED LIFE REALLY IS.

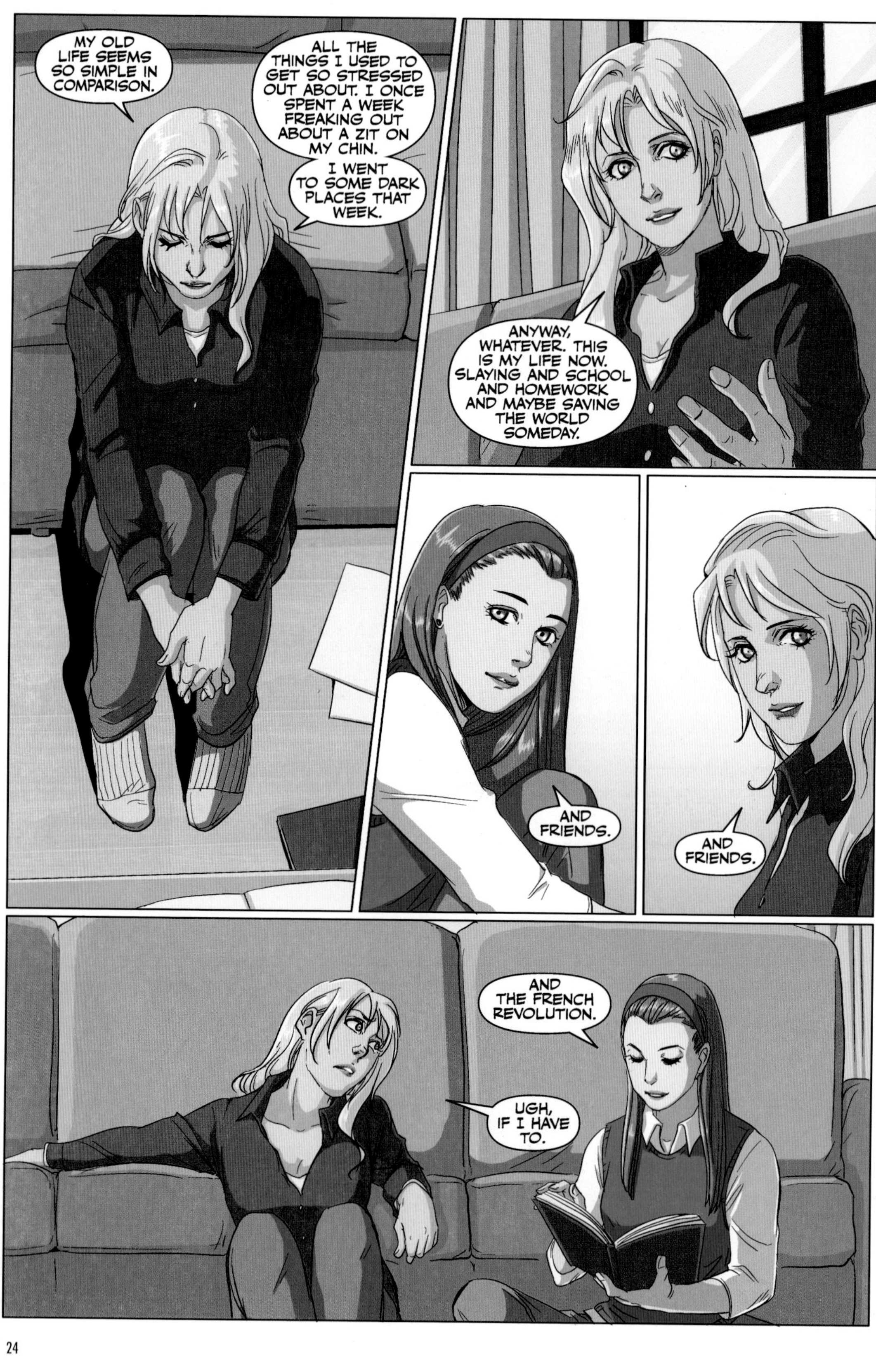
MY OLD LIFE SEEMS SO SIMPLE IN COMPARISON.
ALL THE THINGS I USED TO GET SO STRESSED OUT ABOUT. I ONCE SPENT A WEEK FREAKING OUT ABOUT A ZIT ON MY CHIN.
I WENT TO SOME DARK PLACES THAT WEEK.
ANYWAY, WHATEVER. THIS IS MY LIFE NOW. SLAYING AND SCHOOL AND HOMEWORK AND MAYBE SAVING THE WORLD SOMEDAY.
AND FRIENDS.
AND FRIENDS.
AND THE FRENCH REVOLUTION.
UGH, IF I HAVE TO.

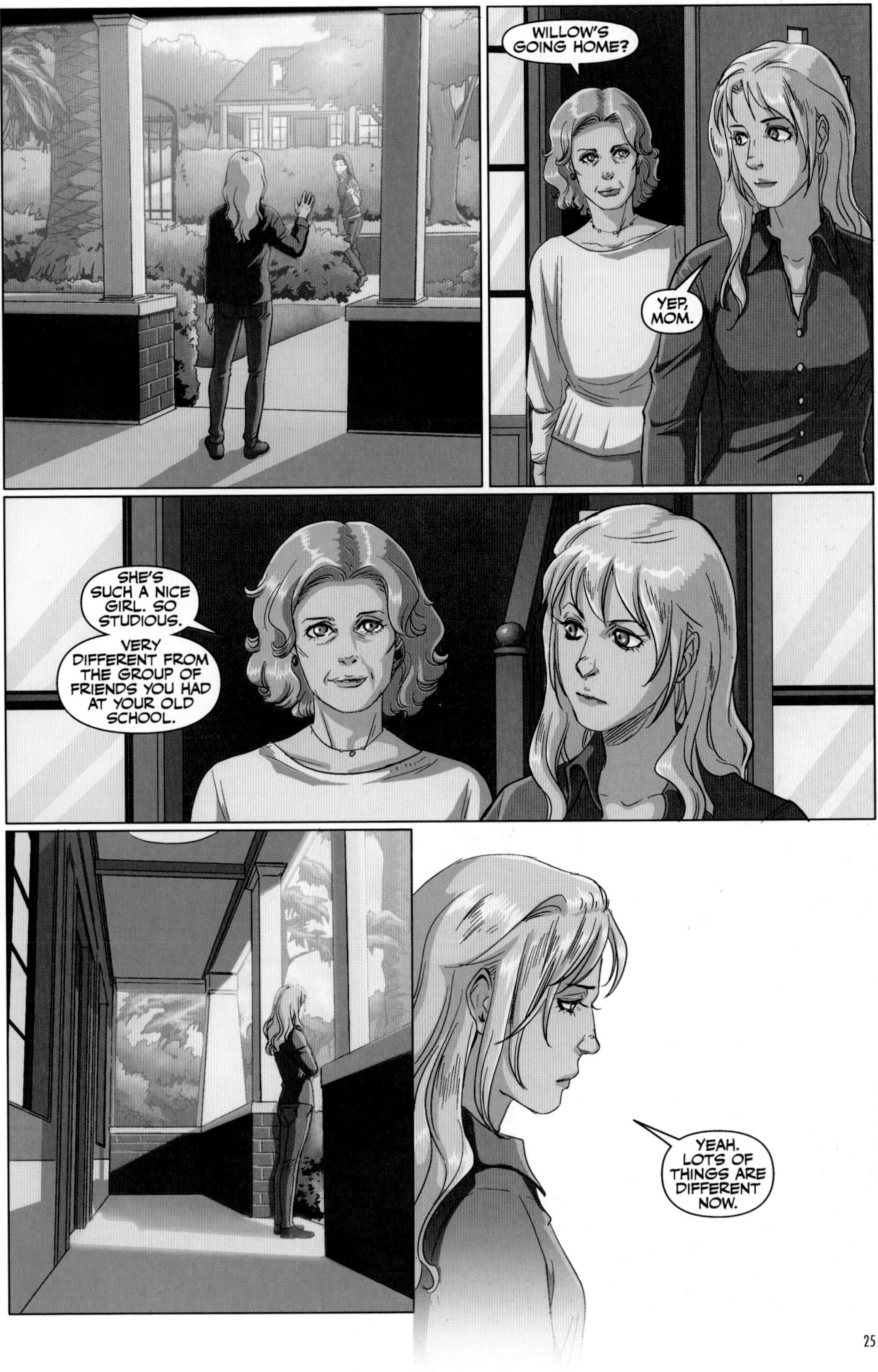
WILLOW'S GOING HOME?
YEP, MOM.
SHE'S SUCH A NICE GIRL. SO STUDIOUS.
VERY DIFFERENT FROM THE GROUP OF FRIENDS YOU HAD AT YOUR OLD SCHOOL.
YEAH. LOTS OF THINGS ARE DIFFERENT NOW.

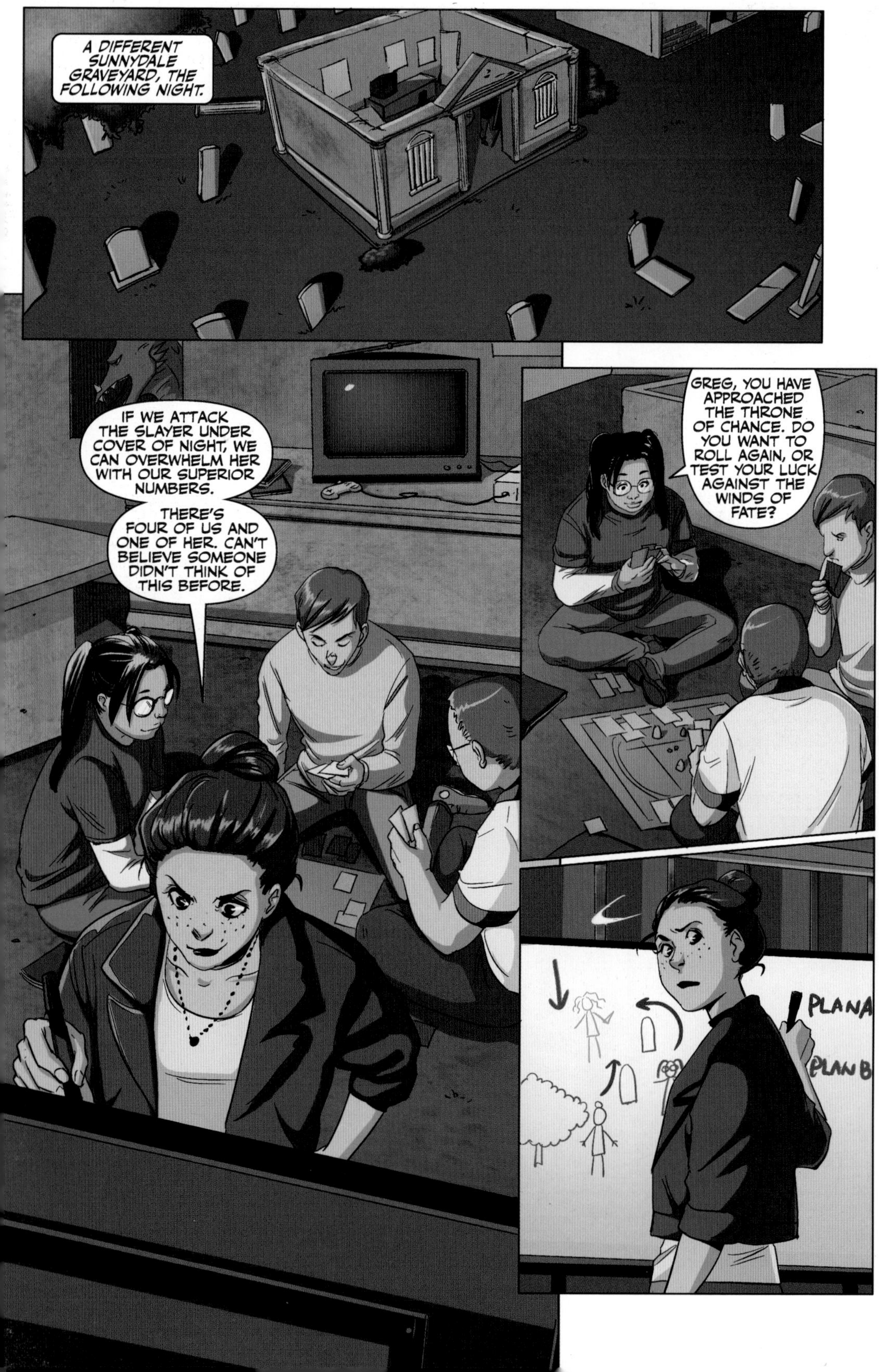
A DIFFERENT SUNNYDALE GRAVEYARD, THE FOLLOWING NIGHT.
IF WE ATTACK THE SLAYER UNDER COVER OF NIGHT, WE CAN OVERWHELM HER WITH OUR SUPERIOR NUMBERS.
THERE'S FOUR OF US AND ONE OF HER. CAN'T BELIEVE SOMEONE DIDN'T THINK OF THIS BEFORE.
GREG, YOU HAVE APPROACHED THE THRONE OF CHANCE. DO YOU WANT TO ROLL AGAIN, OR TEST YOUR LUCK AGAINST THE WINDS OF FATE?
PLAN A
PLAN B

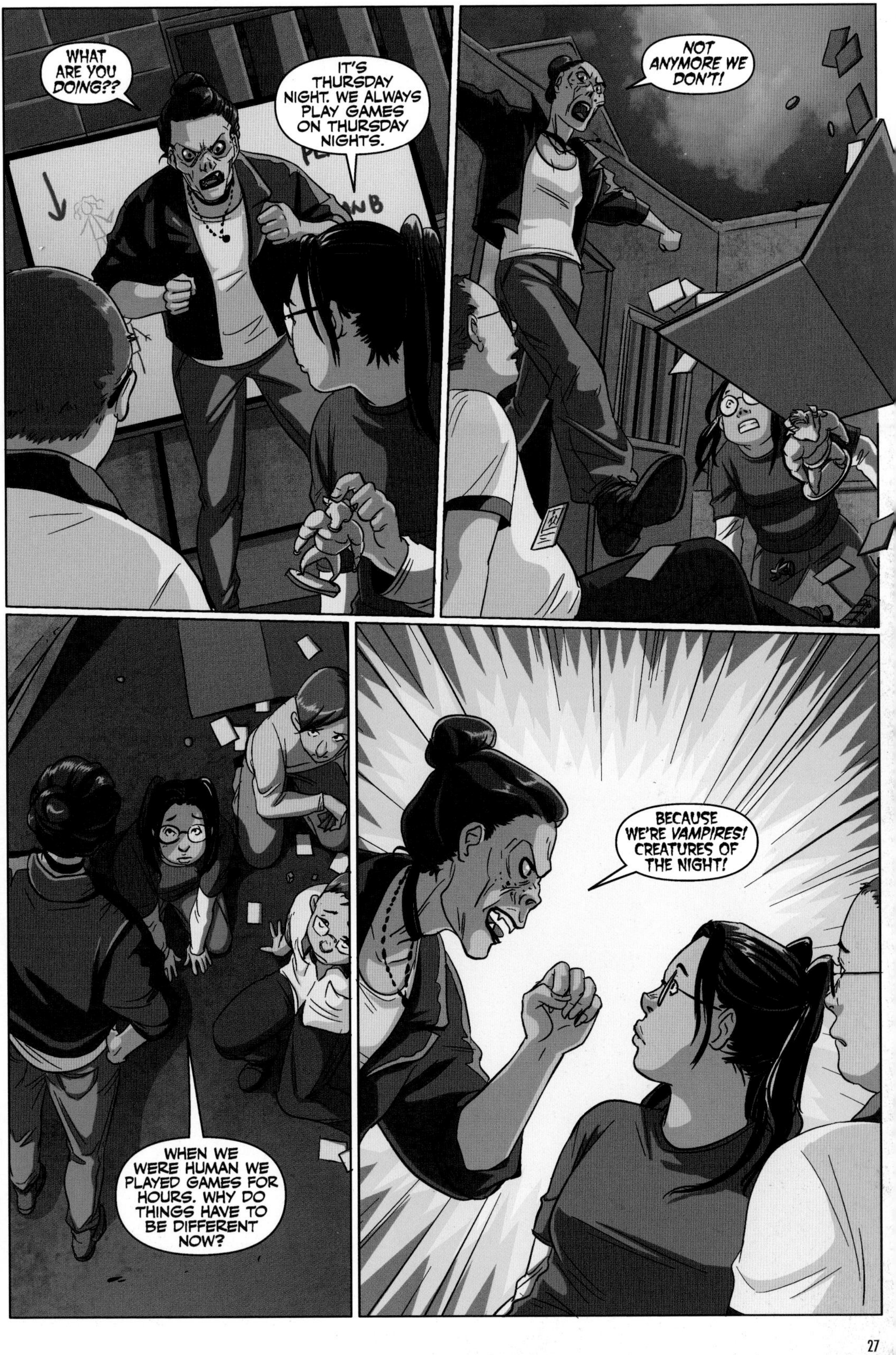
WHAT ARE YOU DOING??
IT'S THURSDAY NIGHT. WE ALWAYS PLAY GAMES ON THURSDAY NIGHTS.
NOT ANYMORE WE DON'T!
BECAUSE WE'RE VAMPIRES! CREATURES OF THE NIGHT!
WHEN WE WERE HUMAN WE PLAYED GAMES FOR HOURS. WHY DO THINGS HAVE TO BE DIFFERENT NOW?

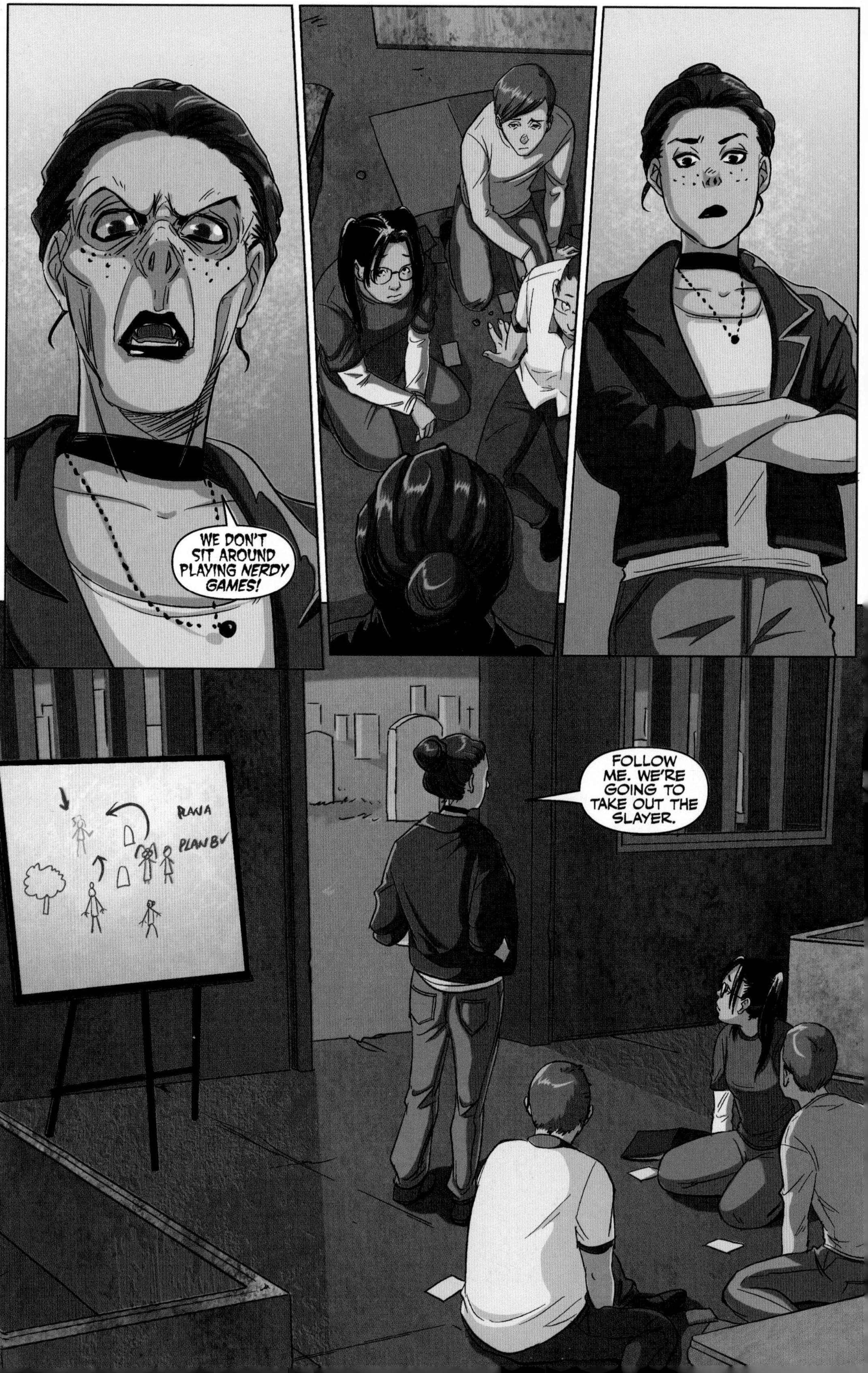
WE DON'T SIT AROUND PLAYING NERDY GAMES!
PLAN B
FOLLOW ME. WE'RE GOING TO TAKE OUT THE SLAYER.

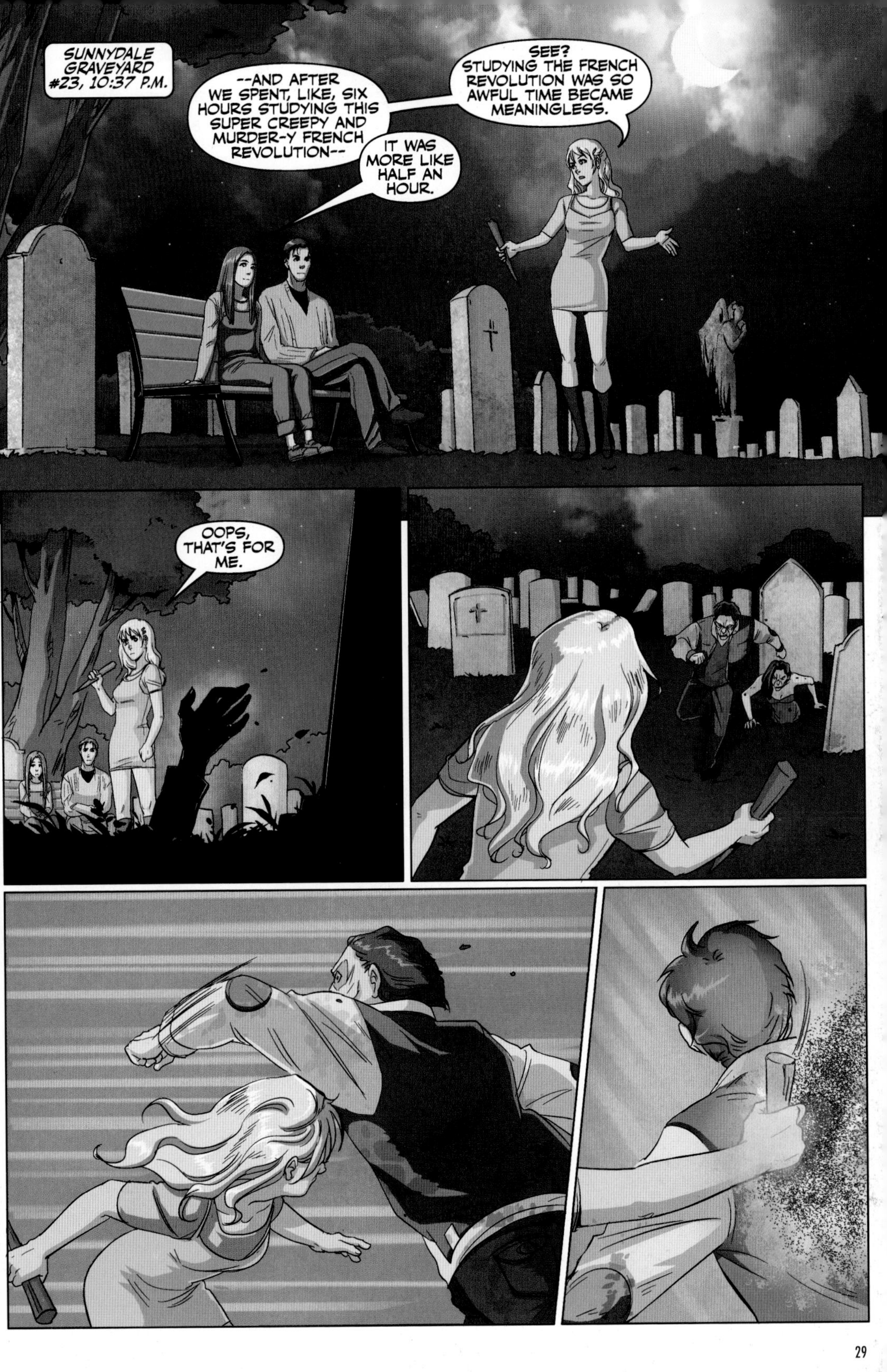
SUNNYDALE GRAVEYARD #23, 10:37 P.M.
--AND AFTER WE SPENT, LIKE, SIX HOURS STUDYING THIS SUPER CREEPY AND MURDER-Y FRENCH REVOLUTION--
IT WAS MORE LIKE HALF AN HOUR.
SEE? STUDYING THE FRENCH REVOLUTION WAS SO AWFUL TIME BECAME MEANINGLESS.
OOPS, THAT'S FOR ME.

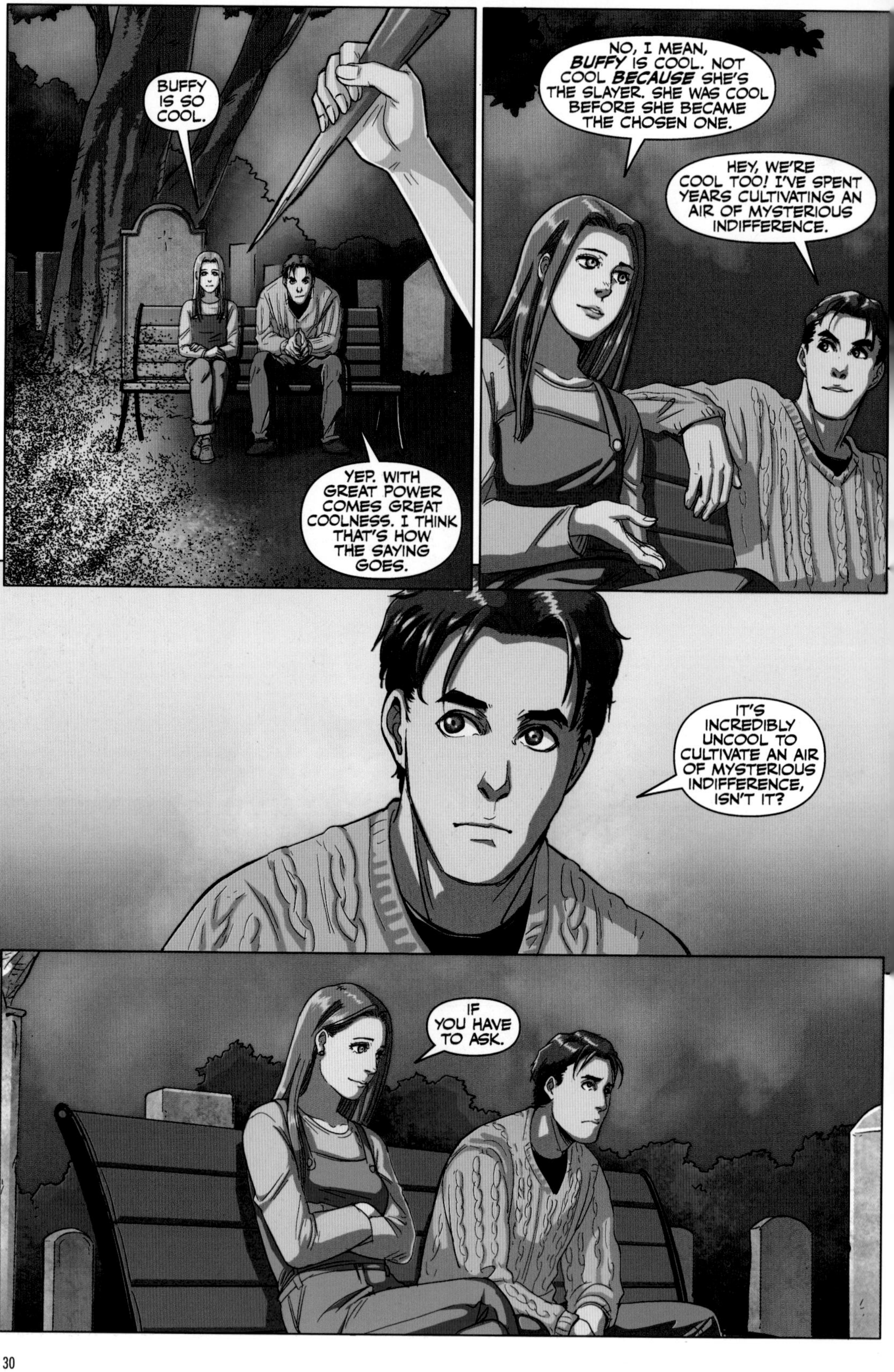
BUFFY IS SO COOL.
YEP. WITH GREAT POWER COMES GREAT COOLNESS. I THINK THAT'S HOW THE SAYING GOES.
NO, I MEAN, BUFFY IS COOL. NOT COOL BECAUSE SHE'S THE SLAYER. SHE WAS COOL BEFORE SHE BECAME THE CHOSEN ONE.
HEY, WE'RE COOL TOO! I'VE SPENT YEARS CULTIVATING AN AIR OF MYSTERIOUS INDIFFERENCE.
IT'S INCREDIBLY UNCOOL TO CULTIVATE AN AIR OF MYSTERIOUS INDIFFERENCE, ISN'T IT?
IF YOU HAVE TO ASK.

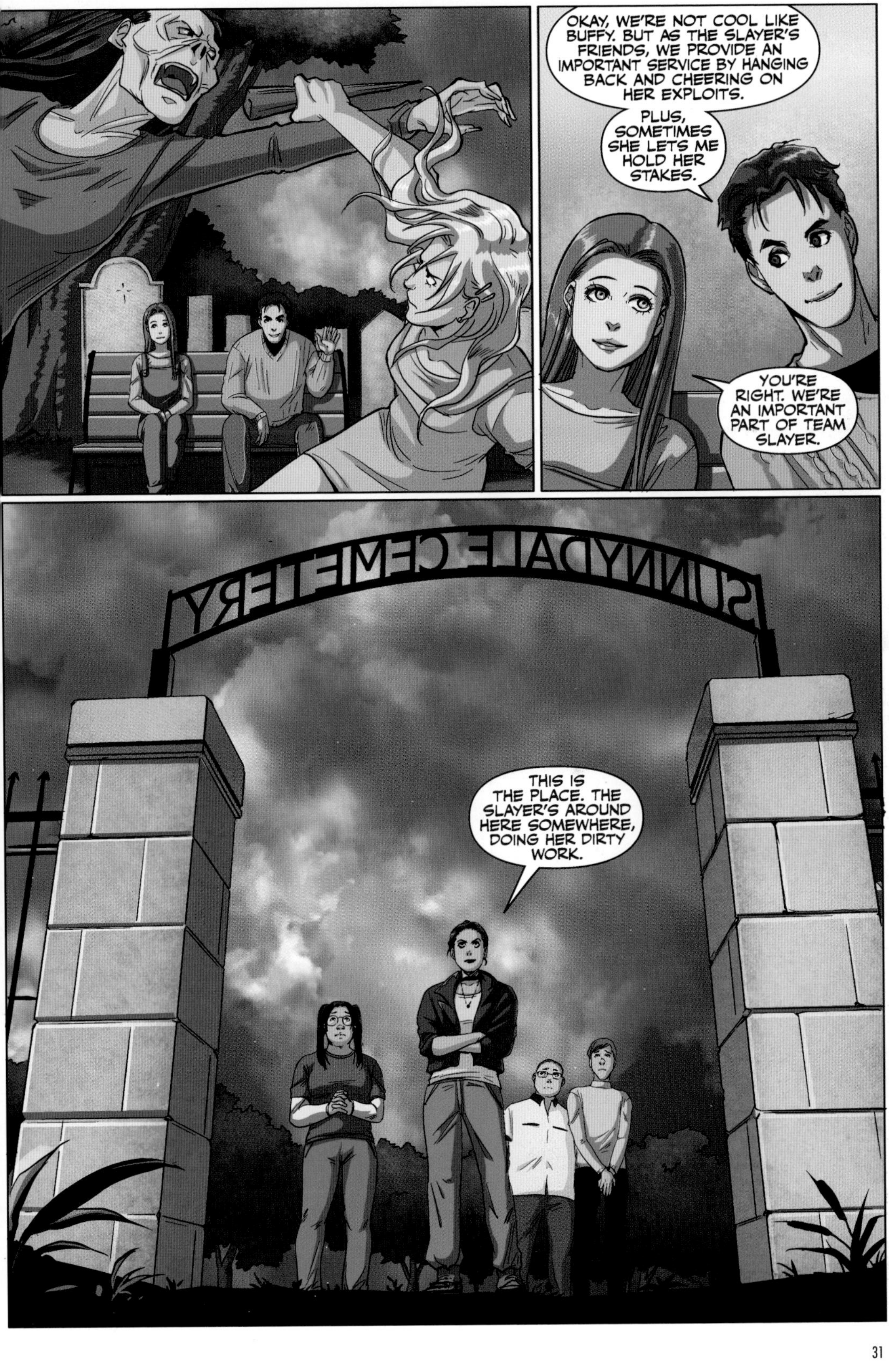
OKAY, WE'RE NOT COOL LIKE BUFFY. BUT AS THE SLAYER'S FRIENDS, WE PROVIDE AN IMPORTANT SERVICE BY HANGING BACK AND CHEERING ON HER EXPLOITS.
PLUS, SOMETIMES SHE LETS ME HOLD HER STAKES.
YOU'RE RIGHT. WE'RE AN IMPORTANT PART OF TEAM SLAYER.
SUNNYDALE CEMETERY
THIS IS THE PLACE. THE SLAYER'S AROUND HERE SOMEWHERE, DOING HER DIRTY WORK.

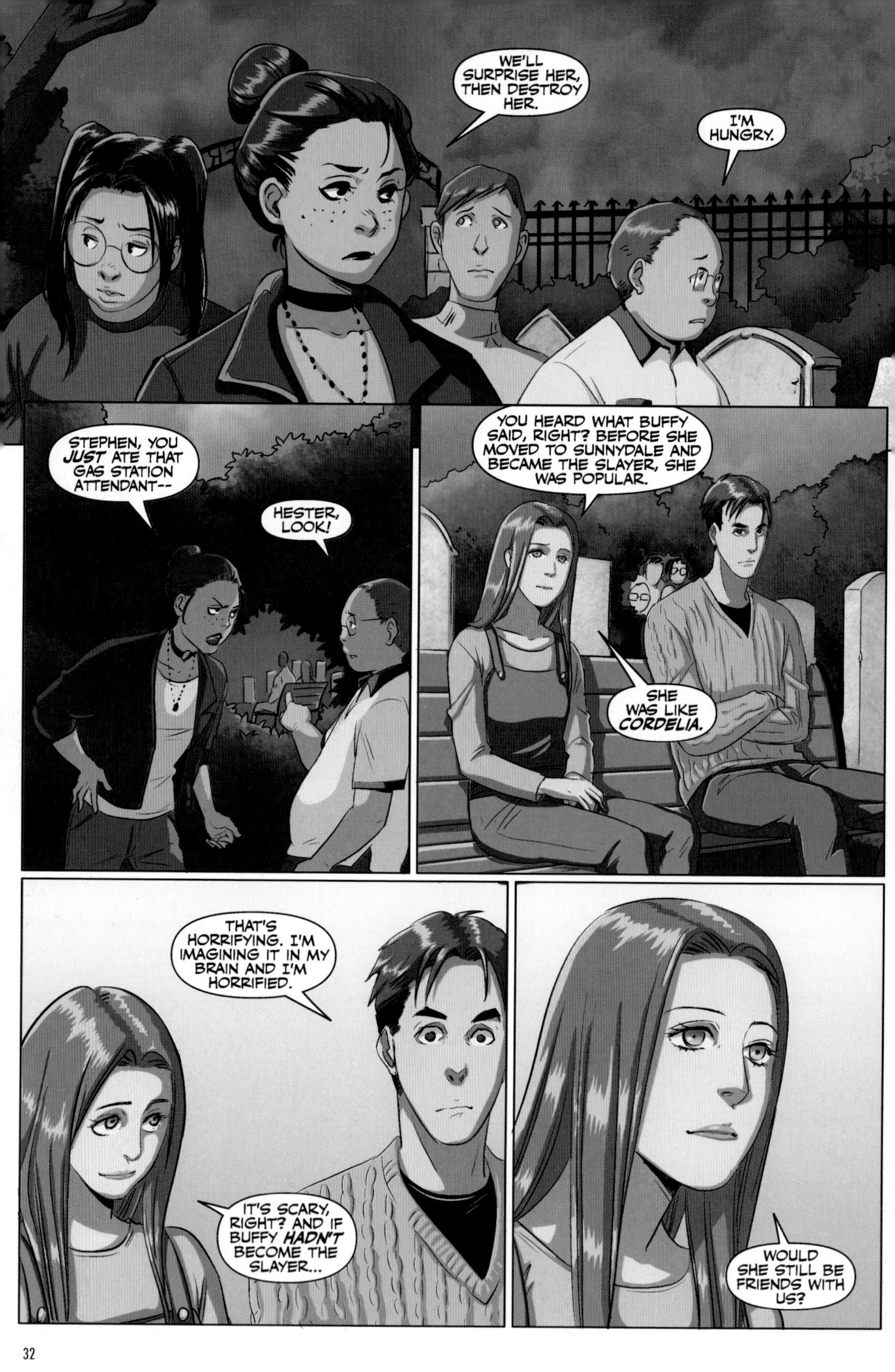
WE'LL SURPRISE HER, THEN DESTROY HER.
I'M HUNGRY.
STEPHEN, YOU JUST ATE THAT GAS STATION ATTENDANT--
HESTER, LOOK!
YOU HEARD WHAT BUFFY SAID, RIGHT? BEFORE SHE MOVED TO SUNNYDALE AND BECAME THE SLAYER, SHE WAS POPULAR.
SHE WAS LIKE CORDELIA.
THAT'S HORRIFYING. I'M IMAGINING IT IN MY BRAIN AND I'M HORRIFIED.
IT'S SCARY, RIGHT? AND IF BUFFY HADN'T BECOME THE SLAYER...
WOULD SHE STILL BE FRIENDS WITH US?

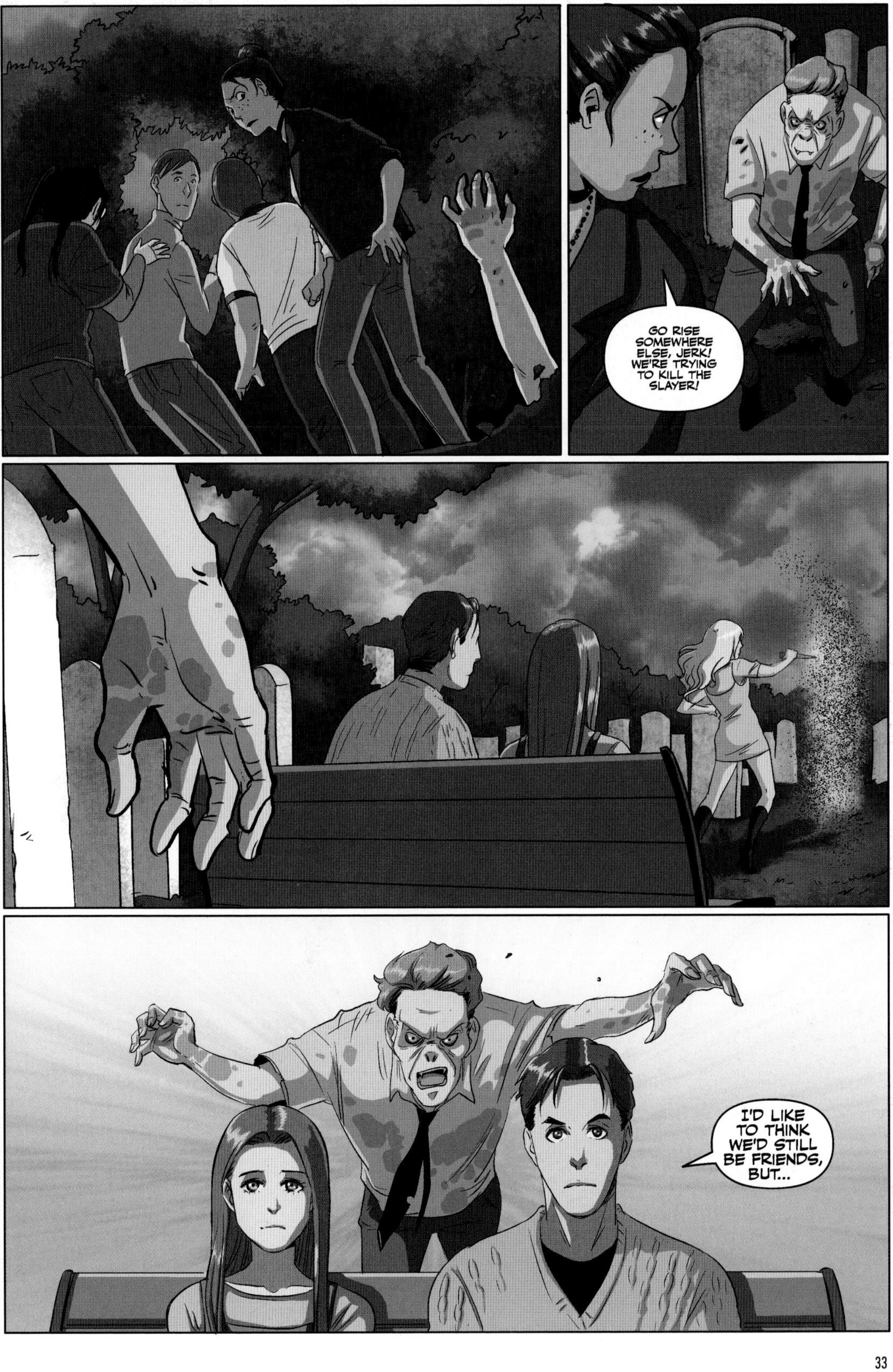
GO RISE SOMEWHERE ELSE, JERK! WE'RE TRYING TO KILL THE SLAYER!
I'D LIKE TO THINK WE'D STILL BE FRIENDS, BUT...

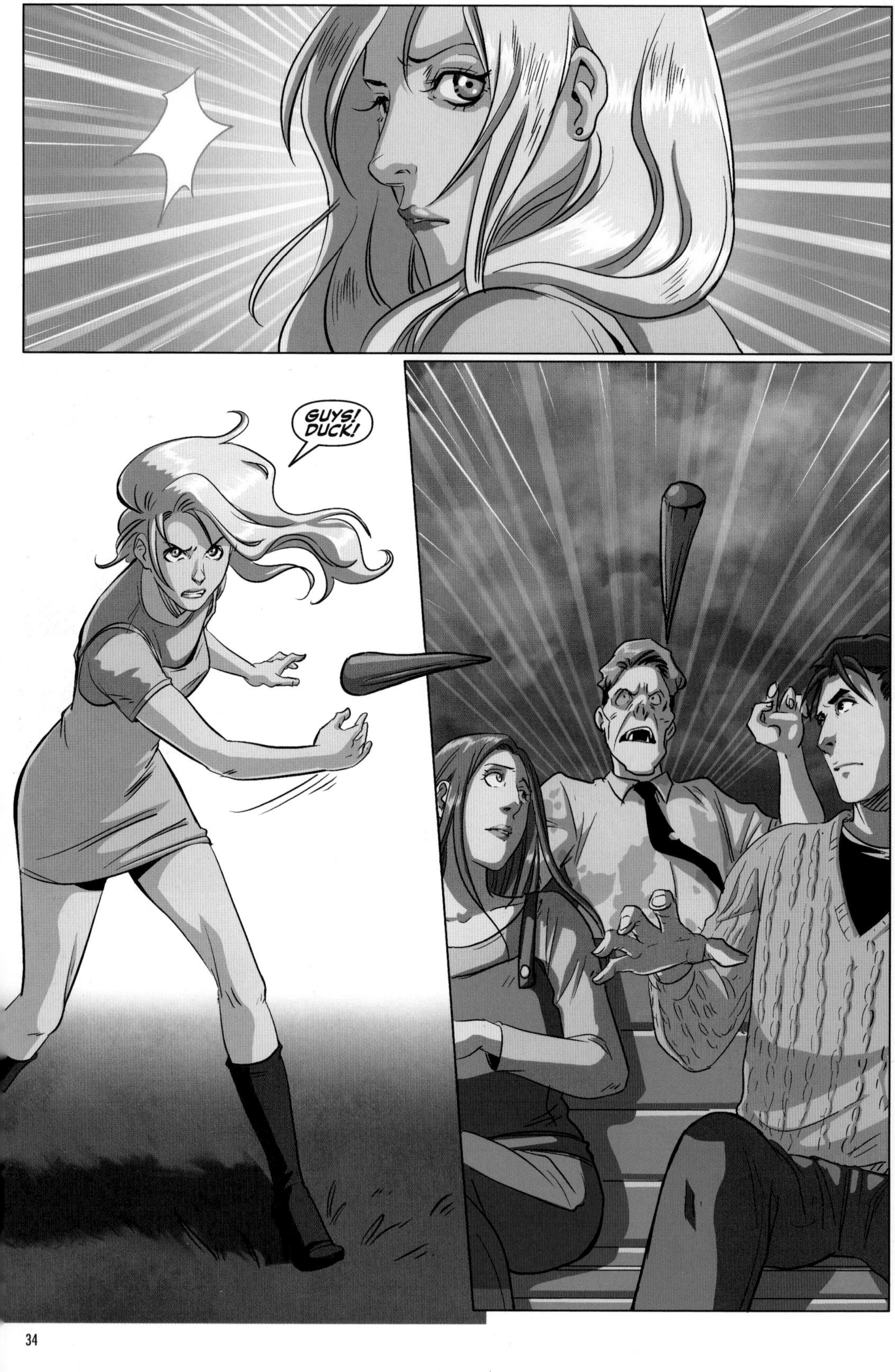
GUYS! DUCK!

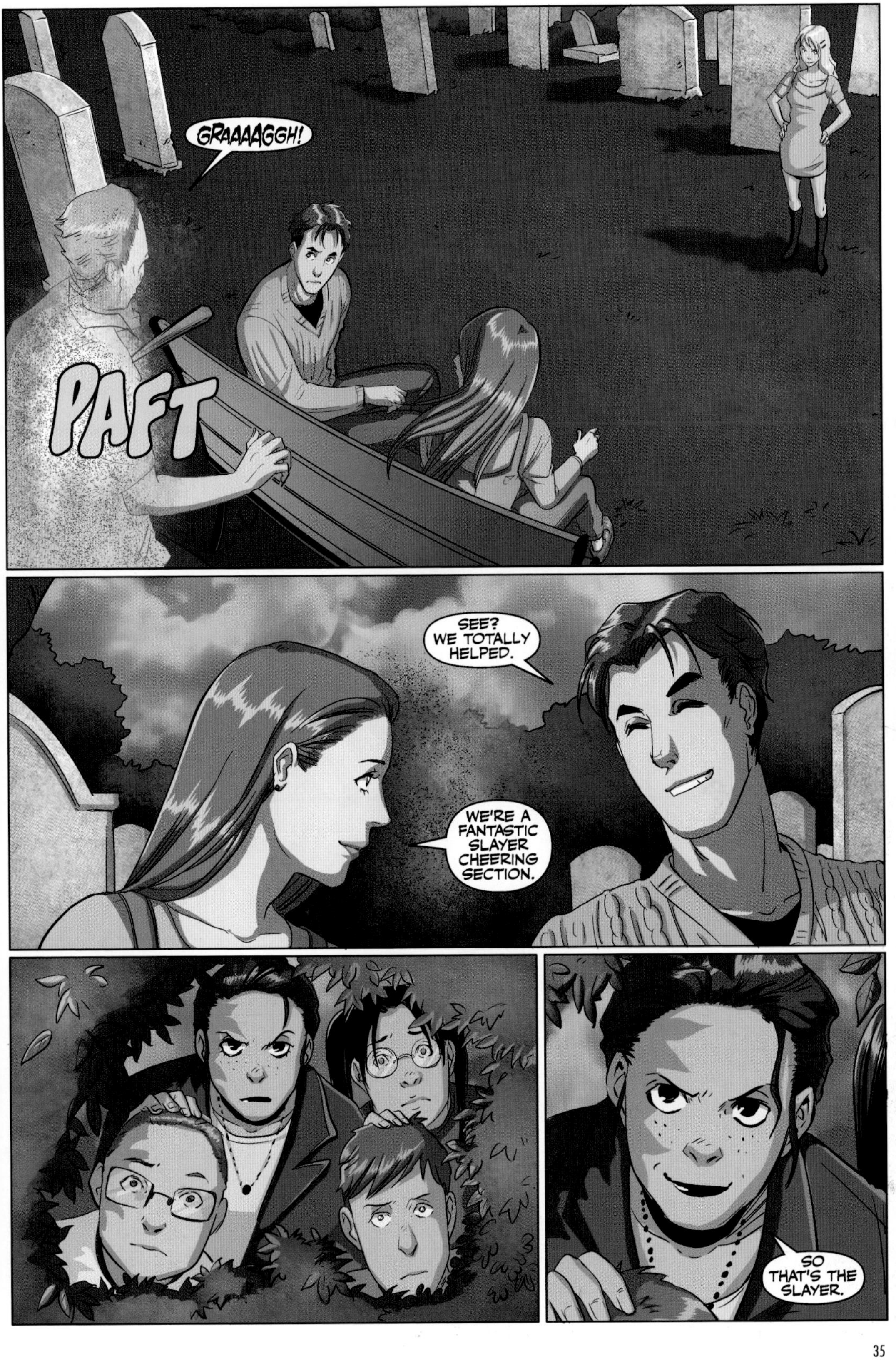
GRAAAAGGH!
PAFT
SEE? WE TOTALLY HELPED.
WE'RE A FANTASTIC SLAYER CHEERING SECTION.
SO THAT'S THE SLAYER.

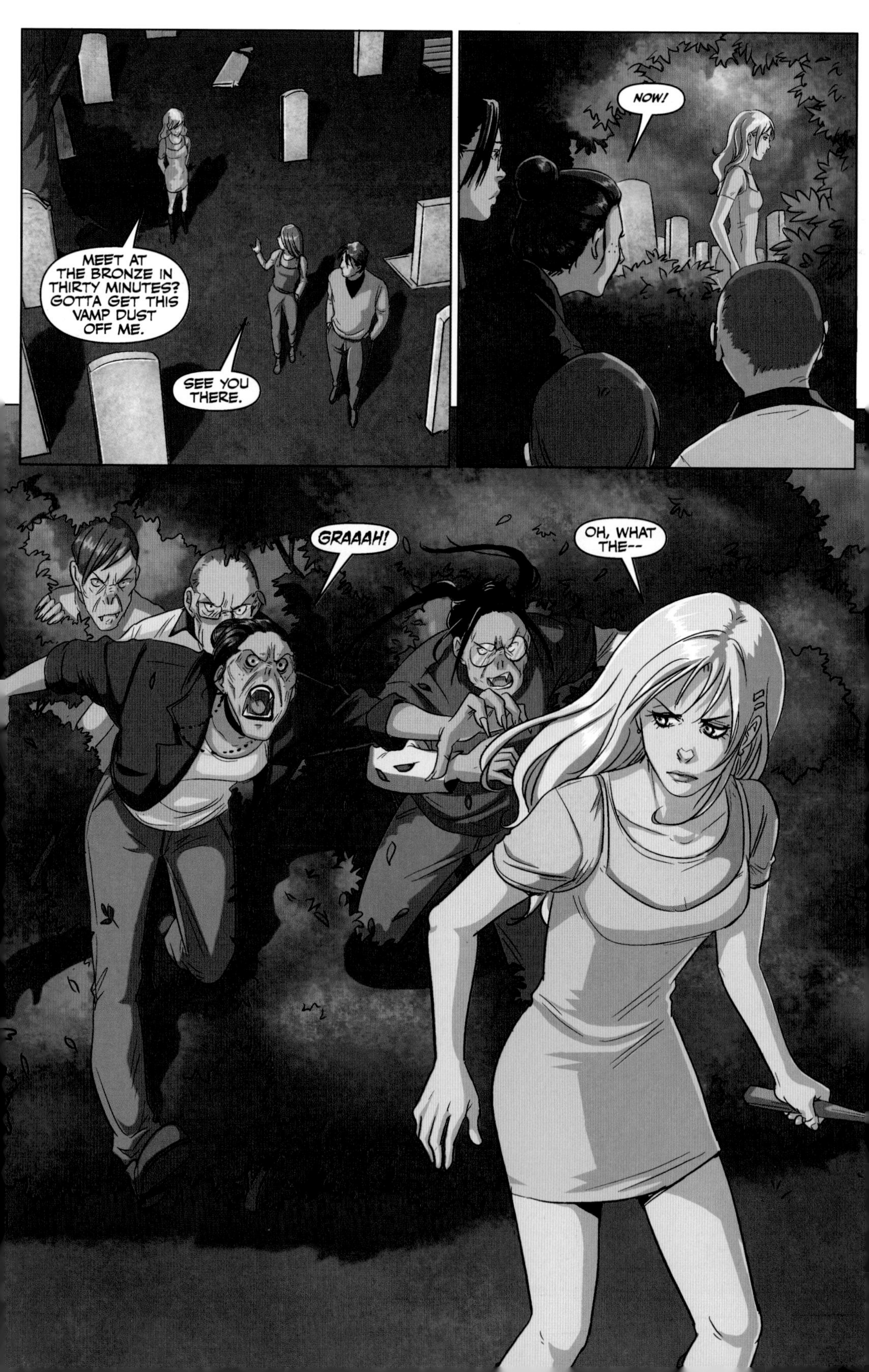
MEET AT THE BRONZE IN THIRTY MINUTES? GOTTA GET THIS VAMP DUST OFF ME.
SEE YOU THERE.
NOW!
GRAAAH!
OH, WHAT THE--

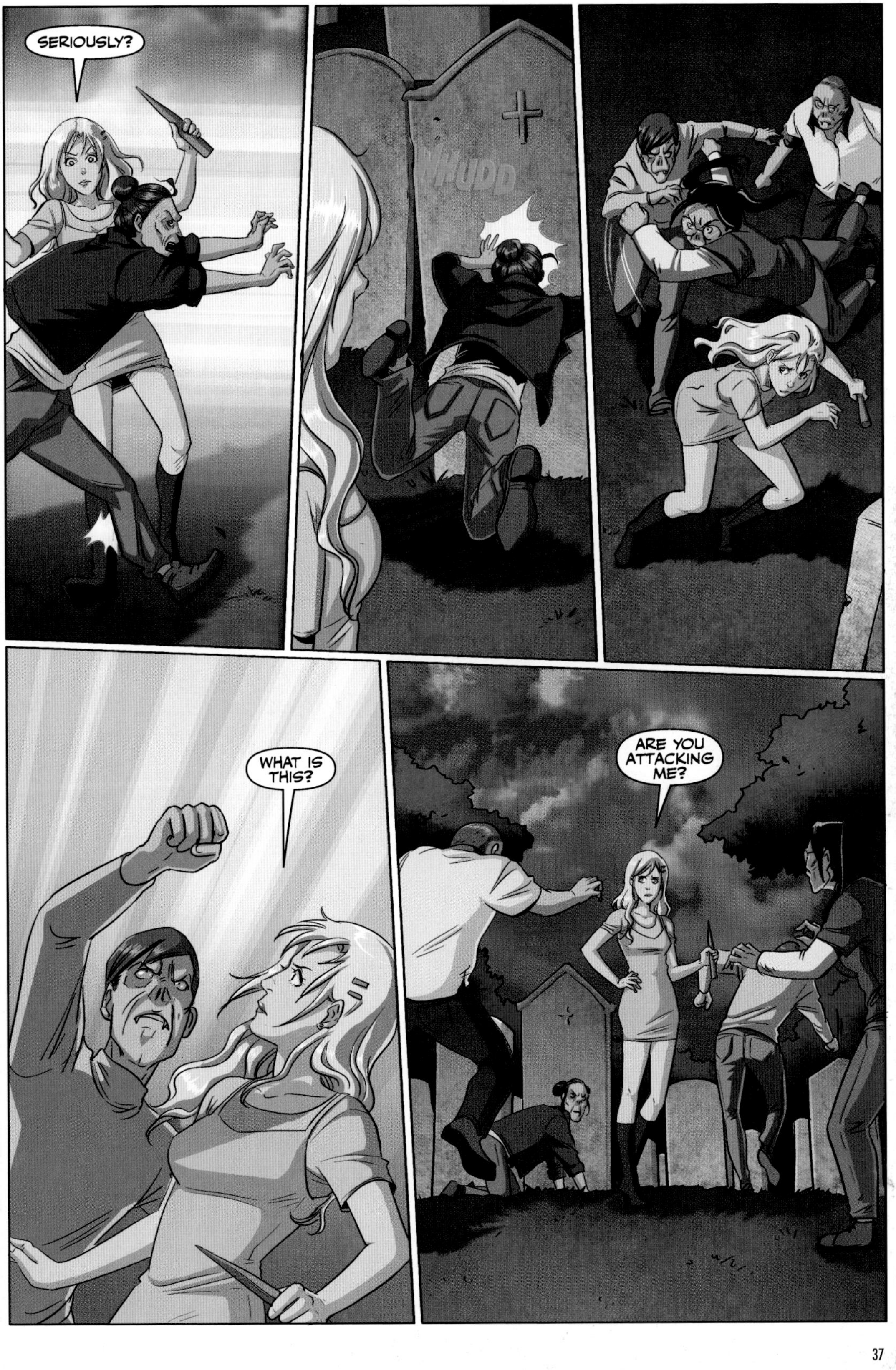
SERIOUSLY?
WHUDD
WHAT IS THIS?
ARE YOU ATTACKING ME?

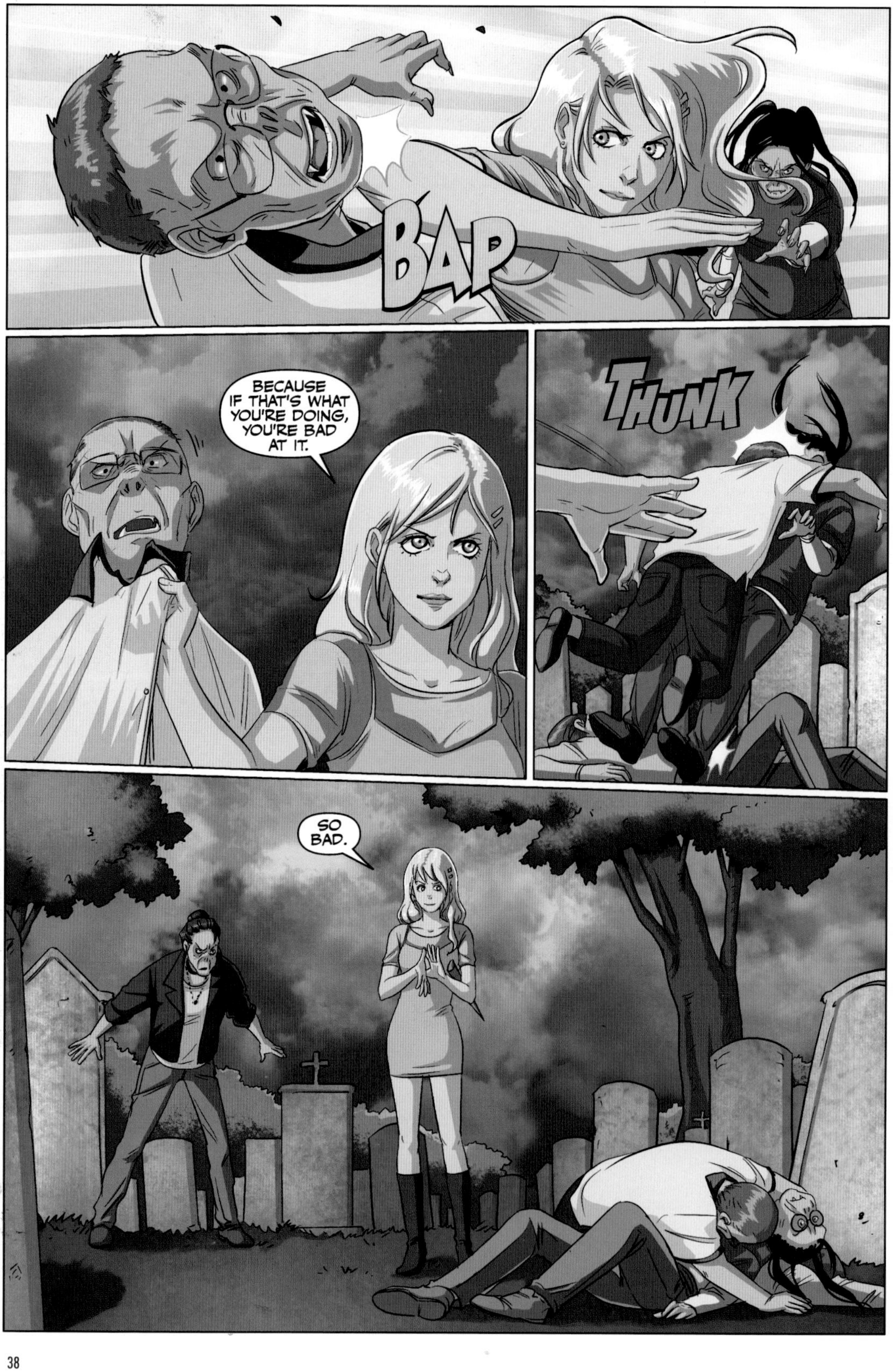
BAP
BECAUSE IF THAT'S WHAT YOU'RE DOING, YOU'RE BAD AT IT.
THUNK
SO BAD.

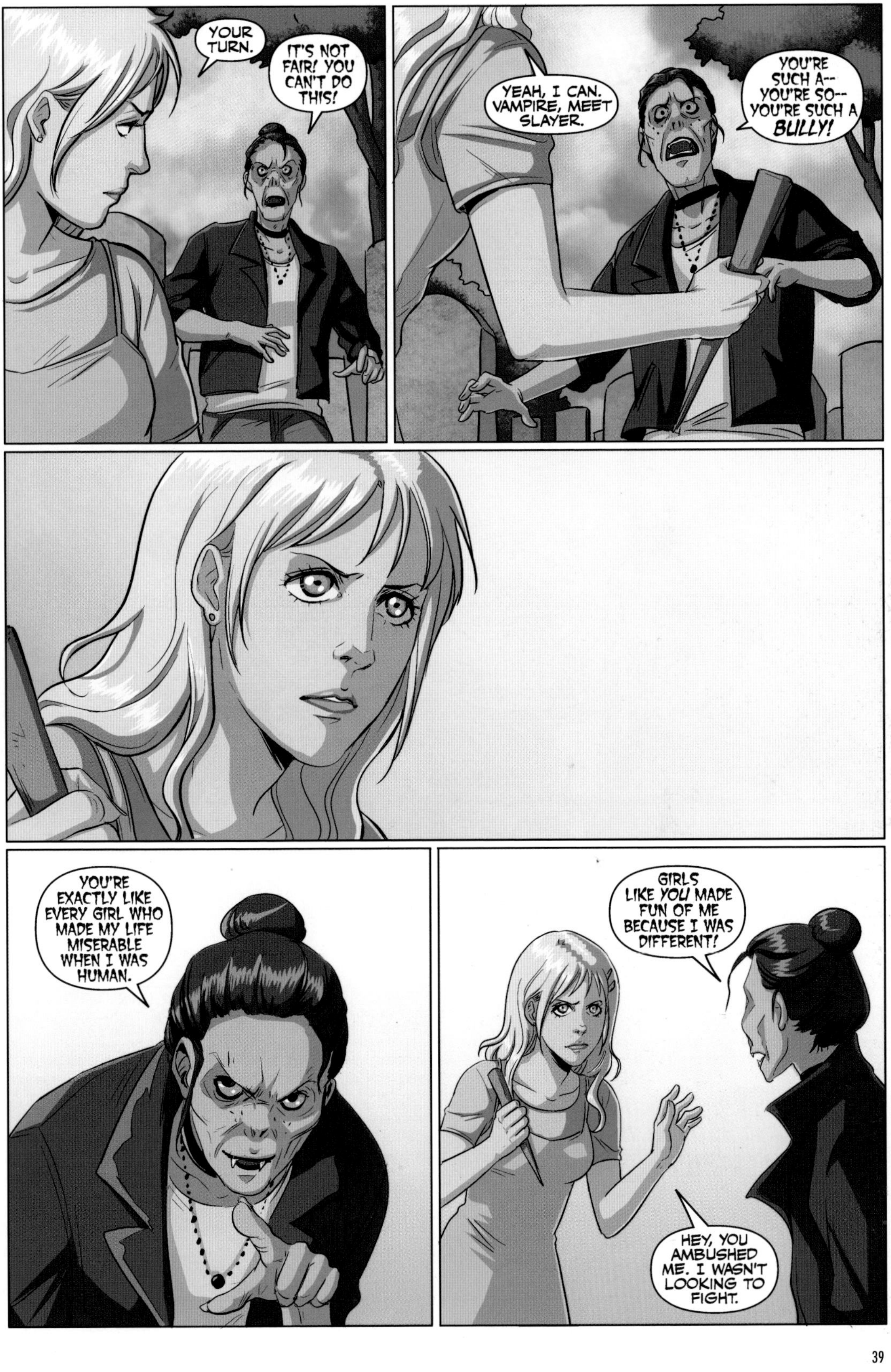
YOUR TURN.
IT'S NOT FAIR! YOU CAN'T DO THIS!
YEAH, I CAN. VAMPIRE, MEET SLAYER.
YOU'RE SUCH A-- YOU'RE SO-- YOU'RE SUCH A *BULLY!*
YOU'RE EXACTLY LIKE EVERY GIRL WHO MADE MY LIFE MISERABLE WHEN I WAS HUMAN.
GIRLS LIKE *YOU* MADE FUN OF ME BECAUSE I WAS DIFFERENT!
HEY, YOU AMBUSHED ME. I WASN'T LOOKING TO FIGHT.

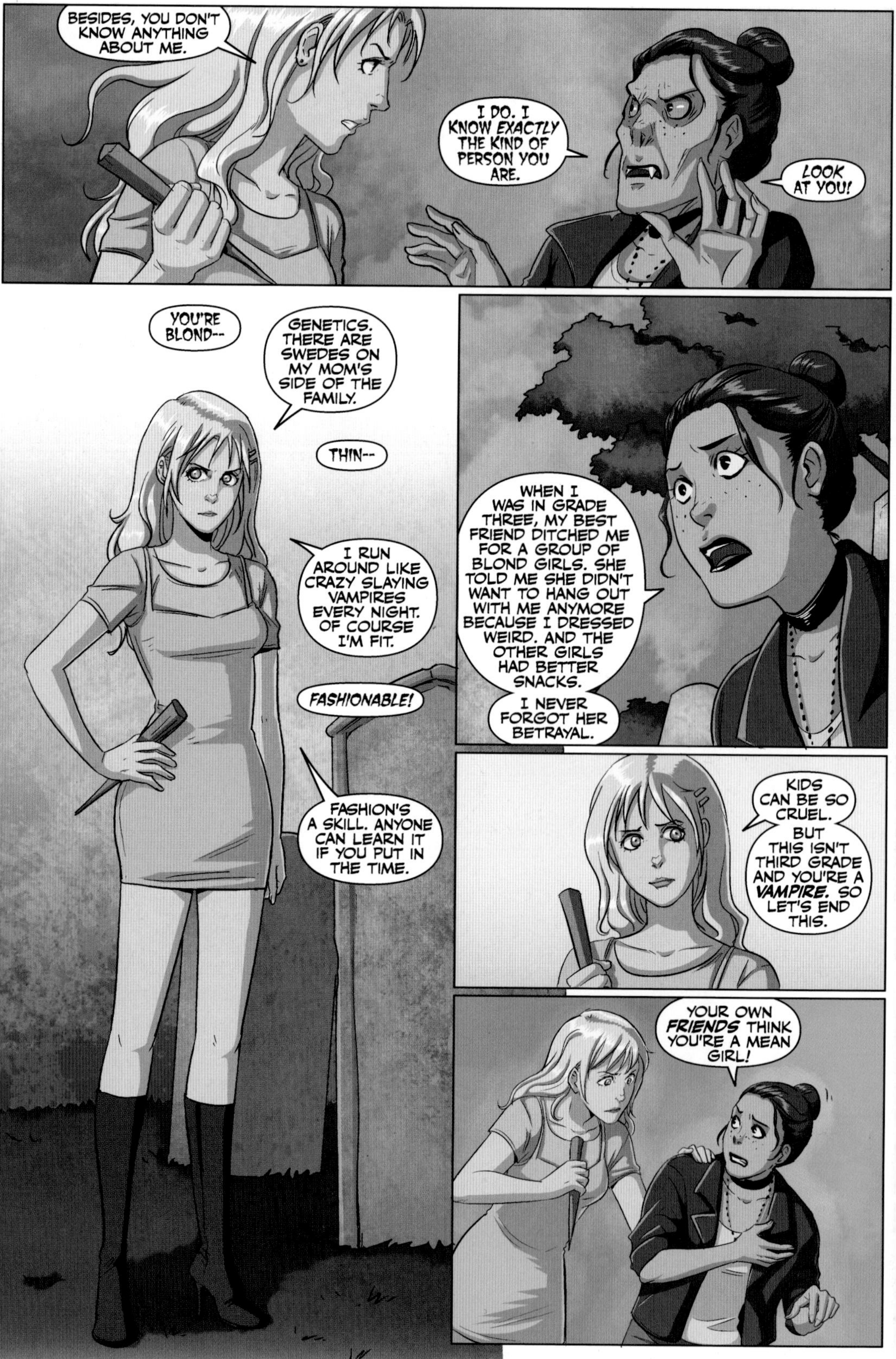

BESIDES, YOU DON'T KNOW ANYTHING ABOUT ME.
I DO. I KNOW *EXACTLY* THE KIND OF PERSON YOU ARE.
LOOK AT YOU!
YOU'RE BLOND--
GENETICS. THERE ARE SWEDES ON MY MOM'S SIDE OF THE FAMILY.
THIN--
I RUN AROUND LIKE CRAZY SLAYING VAMPIRES EVERY NIGHT. OF COURSE I'M FIT.
FASHIONABLE!
FASHION'S A SKILL. ANYONE CAN LEARN IT IF YOU PUT IN THE TIME.
WHEN I WAS IN GRADE THREE, MY BEST FRIEND DITCHED ME FOR A GROUP OF BLOND GIRLS. SHE TOLD ME SHE DIDN'T WANT TO HANG OUT WITH ME ANYMORE BECAUSE I DRESSED WEIRD. AND THE OTHER GIRLS HAD BETTER SNACKS.
I NEVER FORGOT HER BETRAYAL.
KIDS CAN BE SO CRUEL.
BUT THIS ISN'T THIRD GRADE AND YOU'RE A ***VAMPIRE.*** SO LET'S END THIS.
YOUR OWN ***FRIENDS*** THINK YOU'RE A MEAN GIRL!

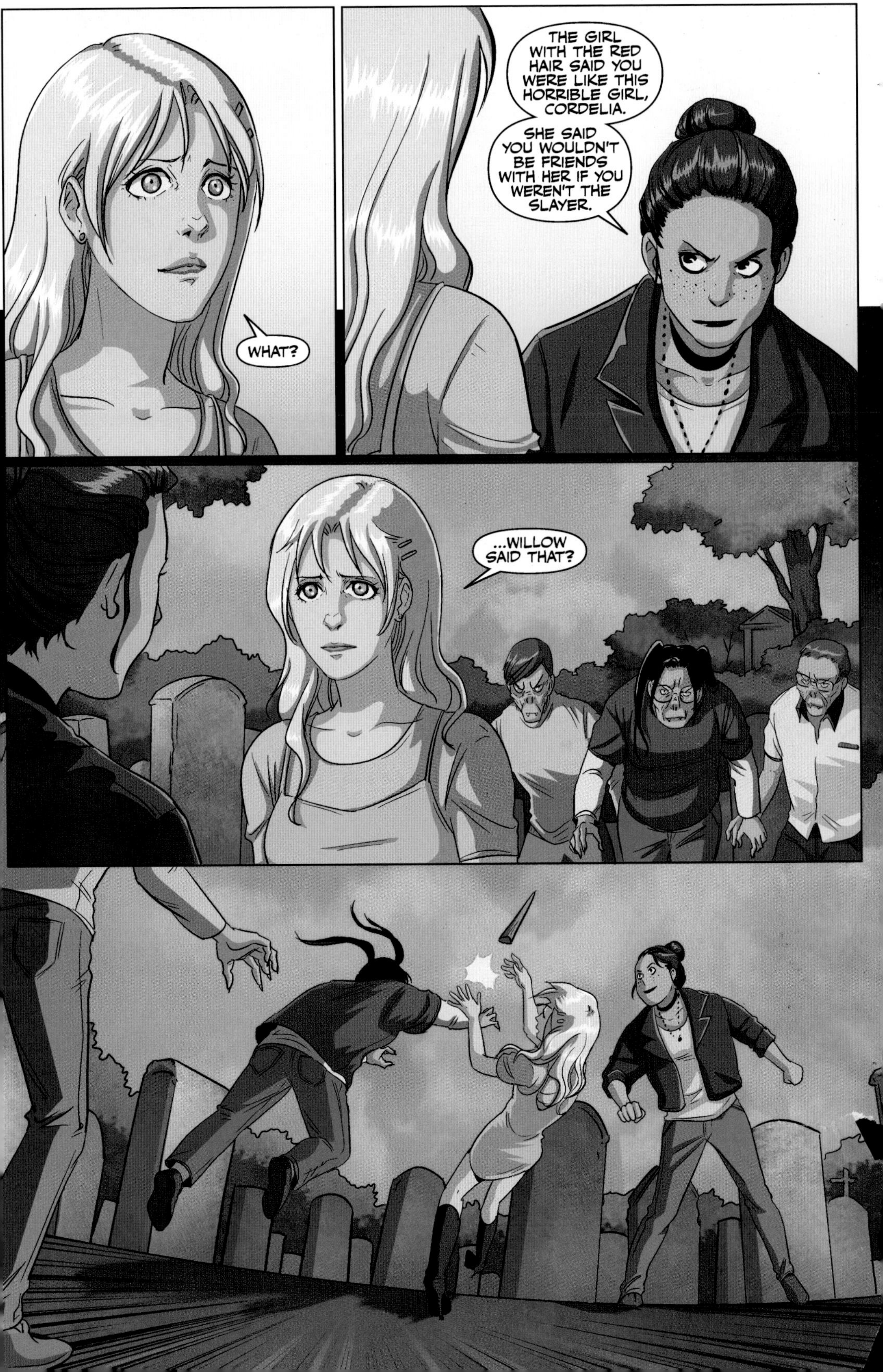
WHAT?
THE GIRL WITH THE RED HAIR SAID YOU WERE LIKE THIS HORRIBLE GIRL, CORDELIA.
SHE SAID YOU WOULDN'T BE FRIENDS WITH HER IF YOU WEREN'T THE SLAYER.
...WILLOW SAID THAT?

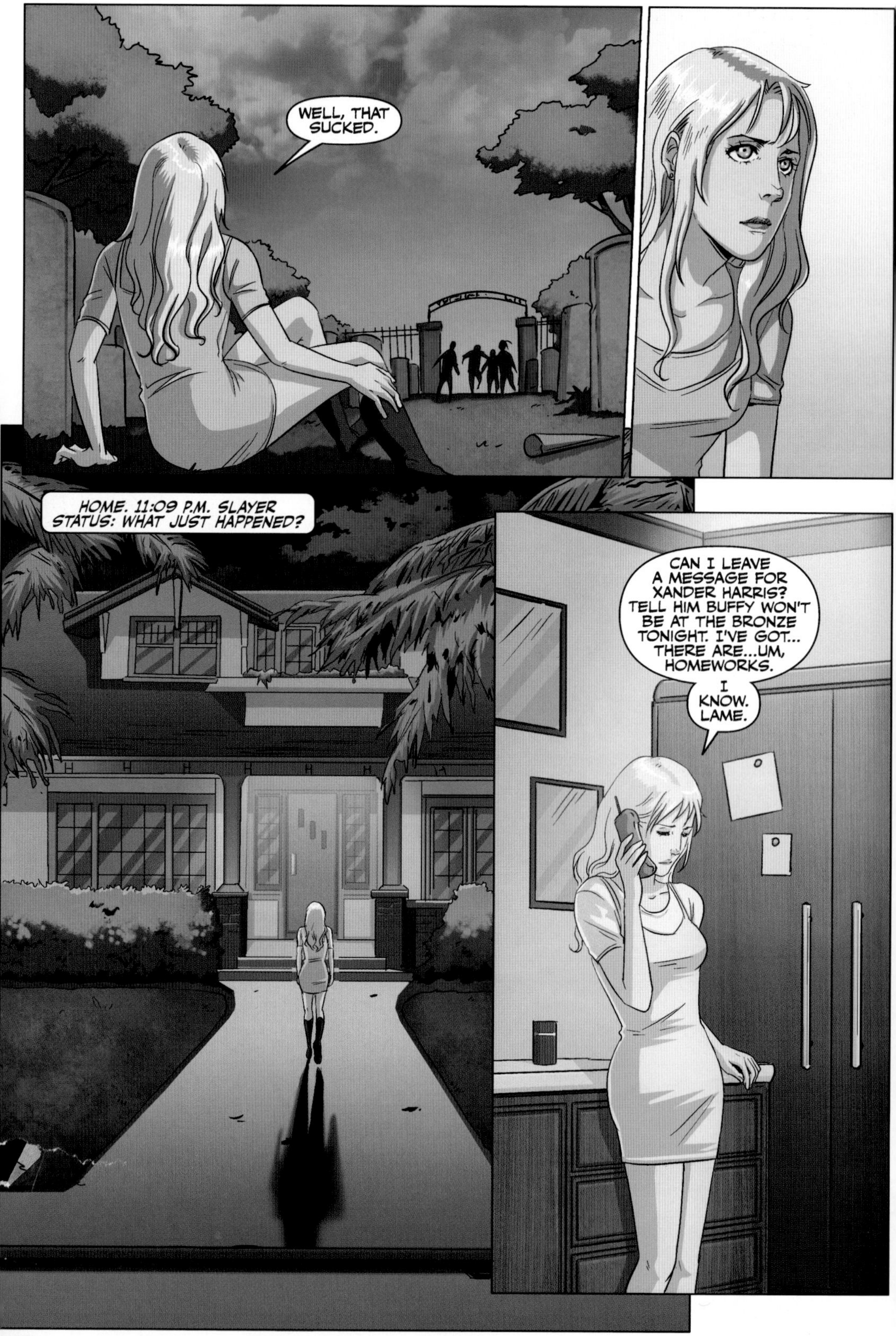
WELL, THAT SUCKED.
HOME. 11:09 P.M. SLAYER STATUS: WHAT JUST HAPPENED?
CAN I LEAVE A MESSAGE FOR XANDER HARRIS? TELL HIM BUFFY WON'T BE AT THE BRONZE TONIGHT. I'VE GOT... THERE ARE...UM, HOMEWORKS.
I KNOW. LAME.

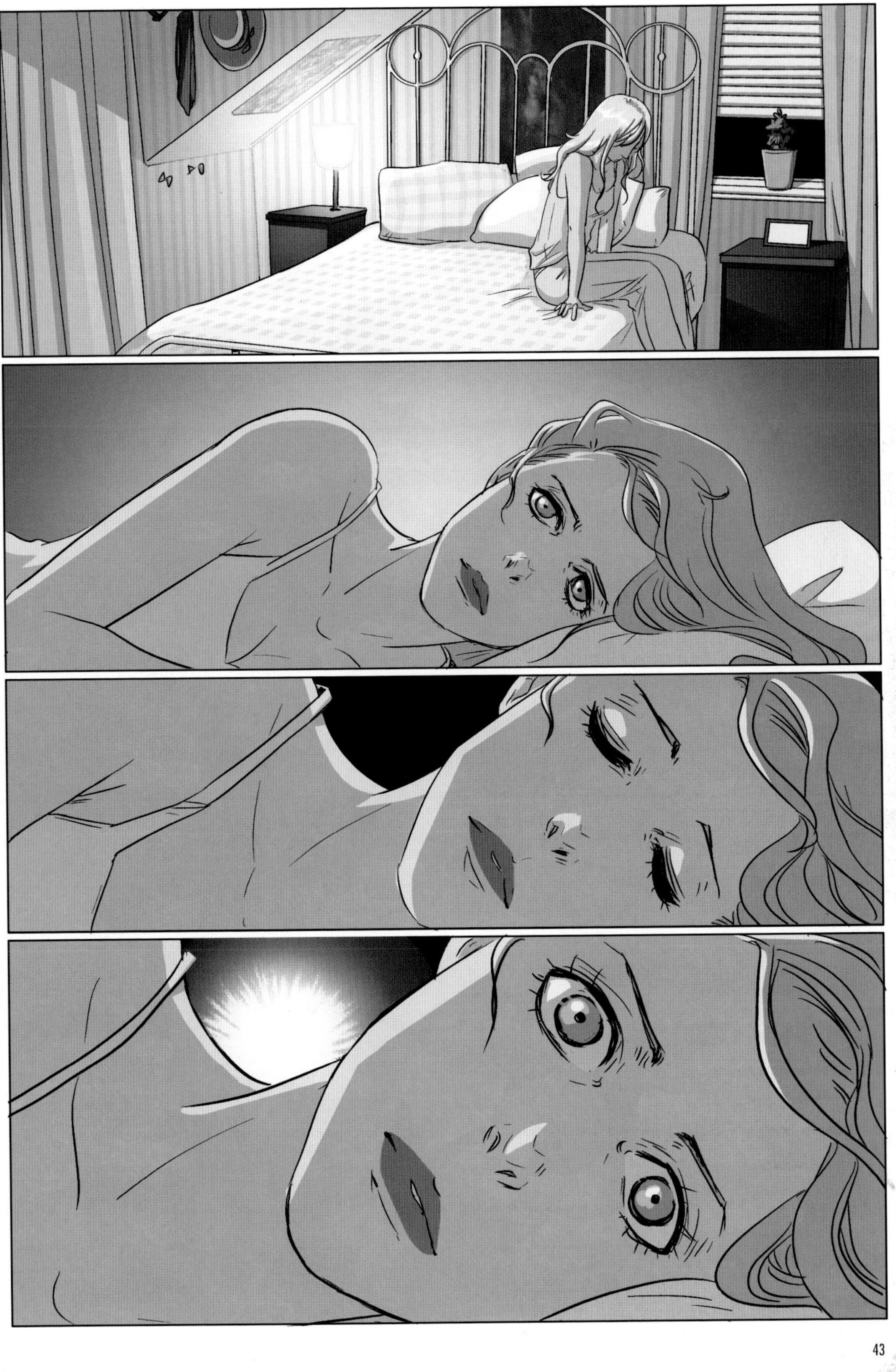

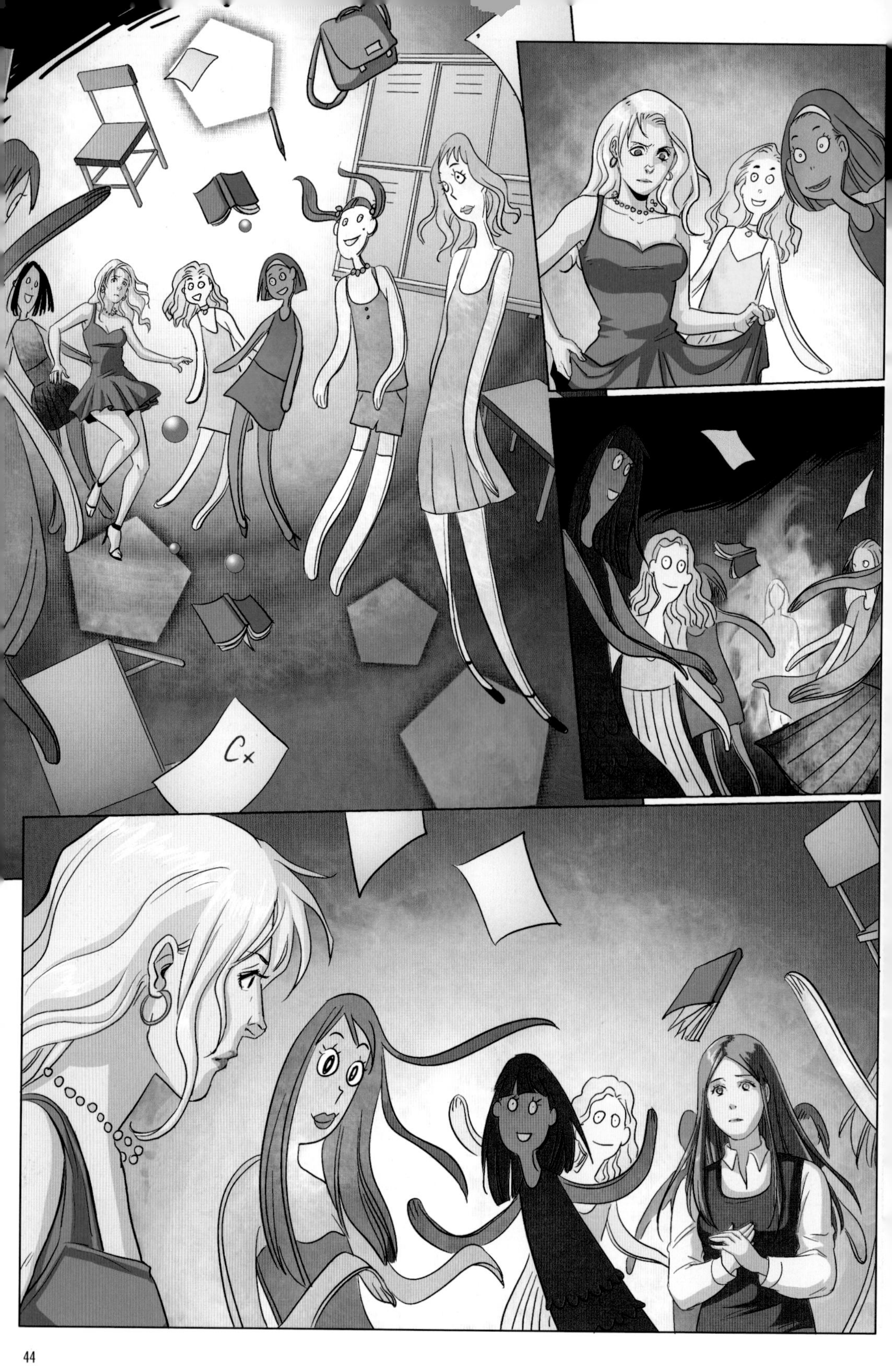
C+

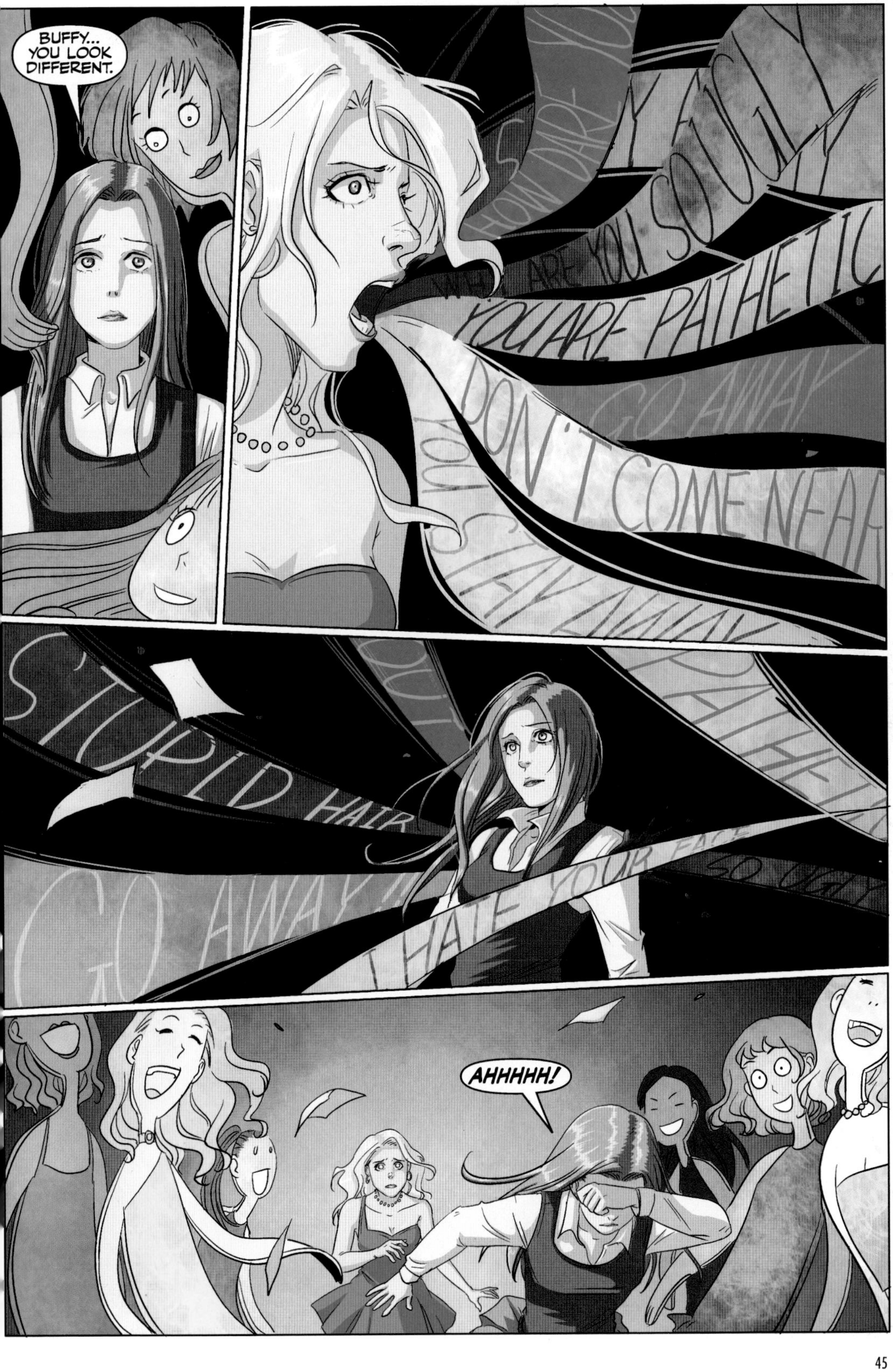
BUFFY... YOU LOOK DIFFERENT.
YOU ARE PATHETIC
DON'T COME NEAR
GO AWAY
STUPID HAIR
GO AWAY!!
I HATE YOUR FACE
AHHHHH!

WHY DID YOU DO THAT? I THOUGHT YOU WERE OUR FRIEND!

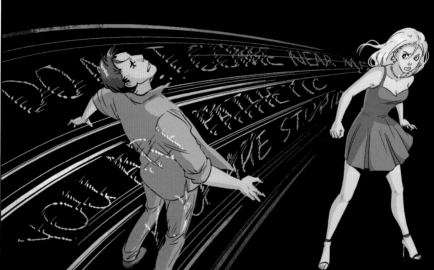

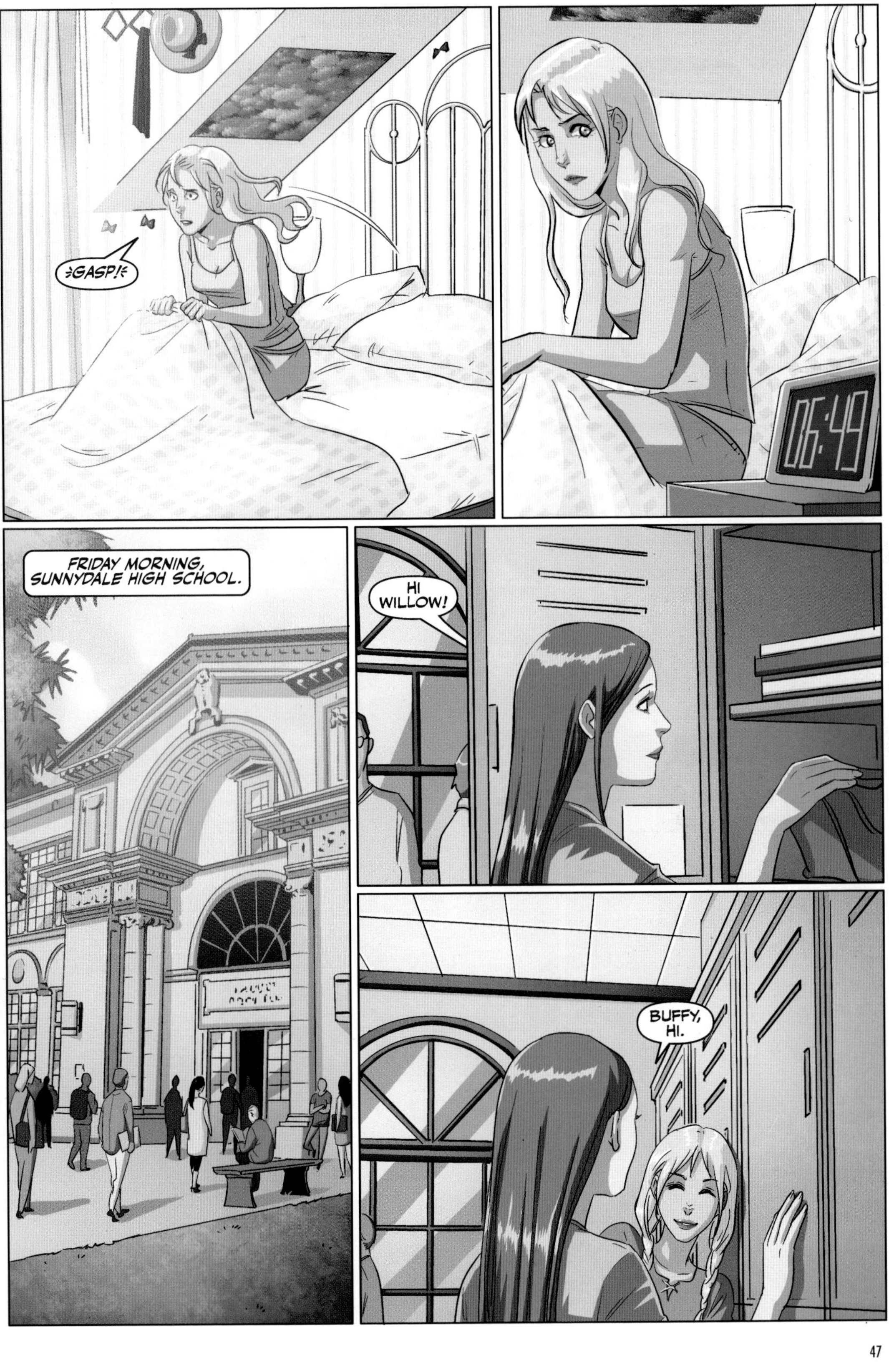
GASP!
06:49
FRIDAY MORNING, SUNNYDALE HIGH SCHOOL.
HI WILLOW!
BUFFY, HI.

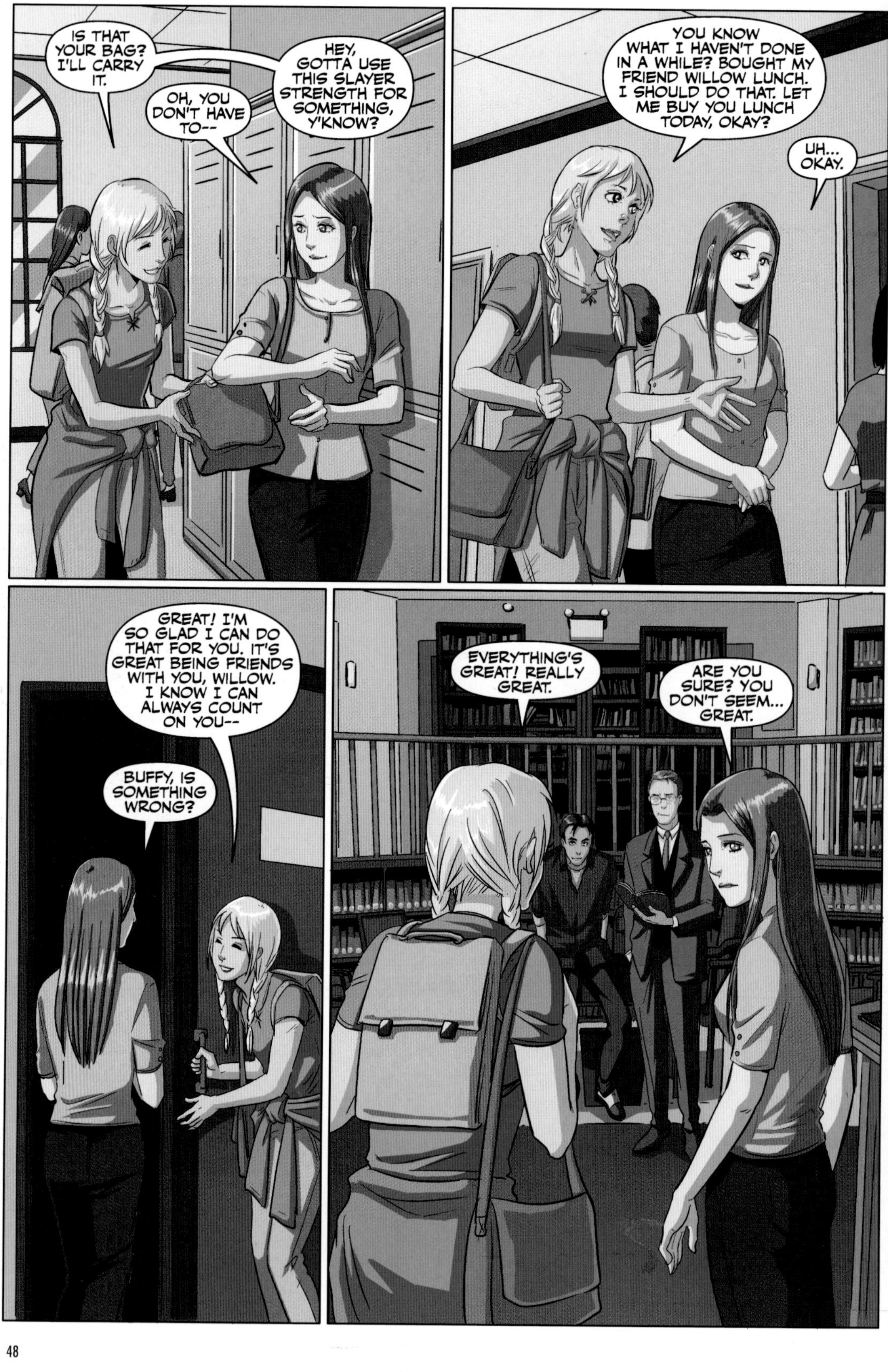
IS THAT YOUR BAG? I'LL CARRY IT.
OH, YOU DON'T HAVE TO--
HEY, GOTTA USE THIS SLAYER STRENGTH FOR SOMETHING, Y'KNOW?
YOU KNOW WHAT I HAVEN'T DONE IN A WHILE? BOUGHT MY FRIEND WILLOW LUNCH. I SHOULD DO THAT. LET ME BUY YOU LUNCH TODAY, OKAY?
UH... OKAY.
GREAT! I'M SO GLAD I CAN DO THAT FOR YOU. IT'S GREAT BEING FRIENDS WITH YOU, WILLOW. I KNOW I CAN ALWAYS COUNT ON YOU--
BUFFY, IS SOMETHING WRONG?
EVERYTHING'S GREAT! REALLY GREAT.
ARE YOU SURE? YOU DON'T SEEM... GREAT.

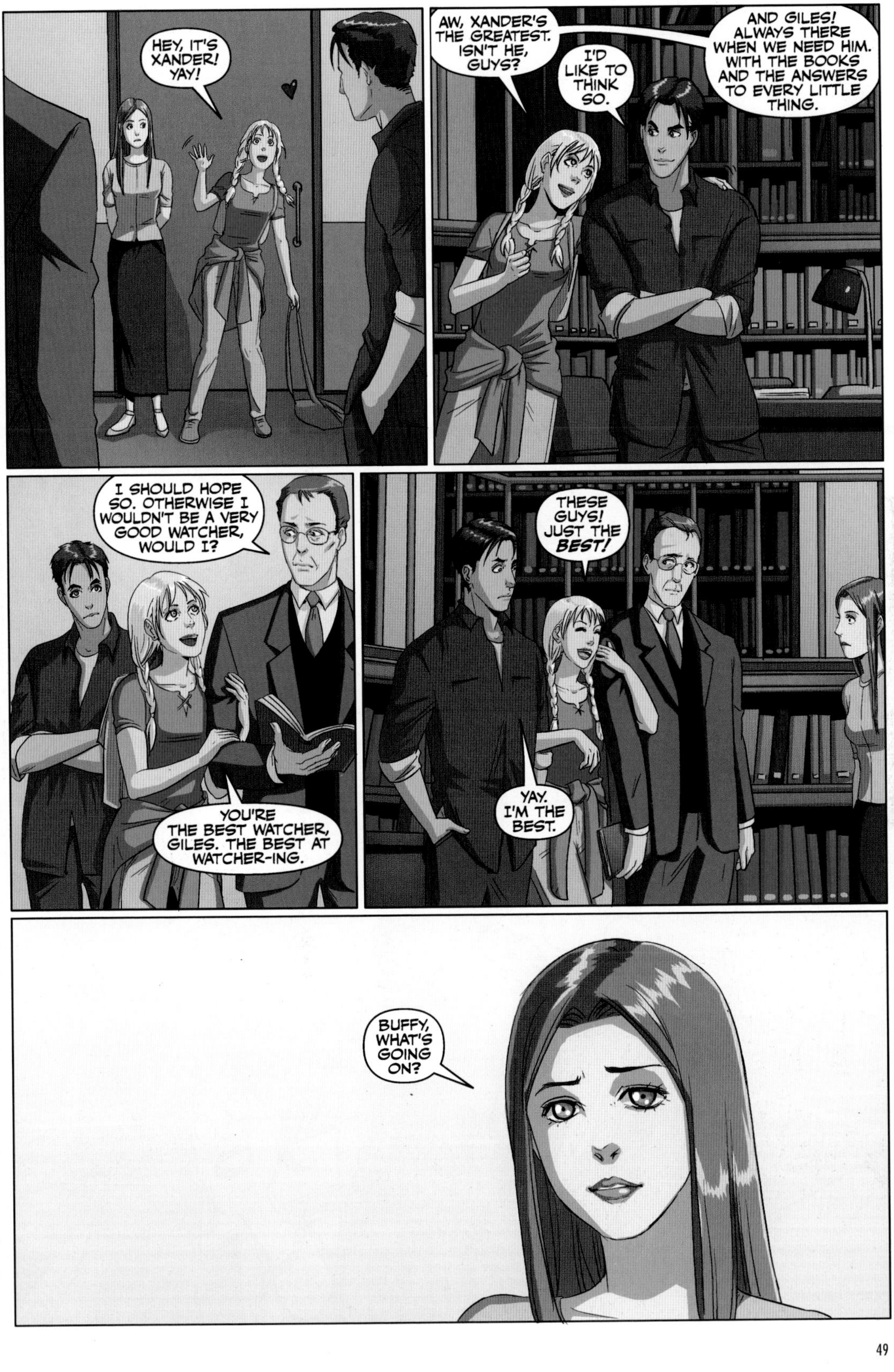

HEY, IT'S XANDER! YAY!
AW, XANDER'S THE GREATEST. ISN'T HE, GUYS?
I'D LIKE TO THINK SO.
AND GILES! ALWAYS THERE WHEN WE NEED HIM. WITH THE BOOKS AND THE ANSWERS TO EVERY LITTLE THING.
I SHOULD HOPE SO. OTHERWISE I WOULDN'T BE A VERY GOOD WATCHER, WOULD I?
YOU'RE THE BEST WATCHER, GILES. THE BEST AT WATCHER-ING.
THESE GUYS! JUST THE *BEST!*
YAY. I'M THE BEST.
BUFFY, WHAT'S GOING ON?

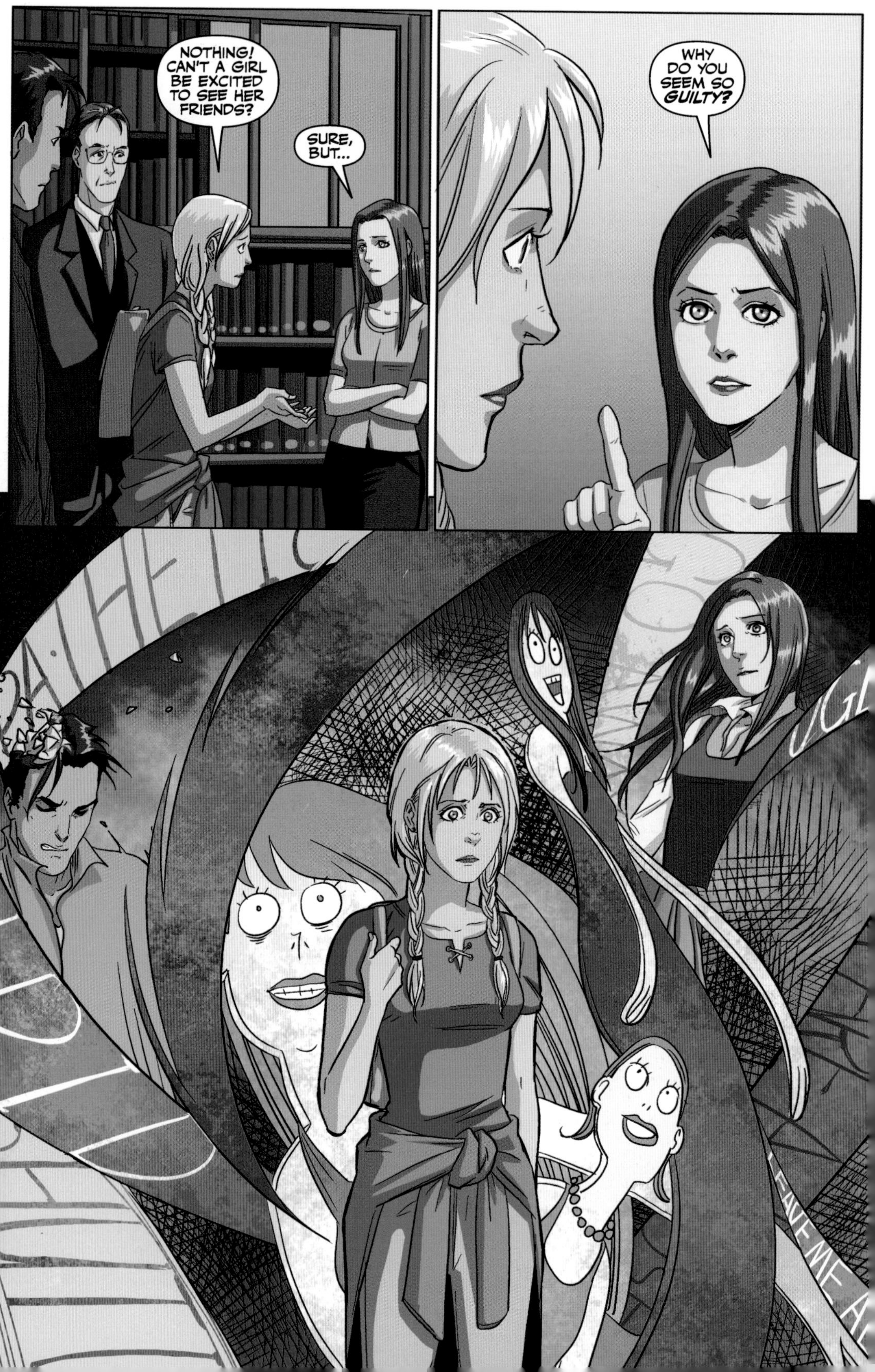
NOTHING! CAN'T A GIRL BE EXCITED TO SEE HER FRIENDS?
SURE, BUT...
WHY DO YOU SEEM SO *GUILTY?*

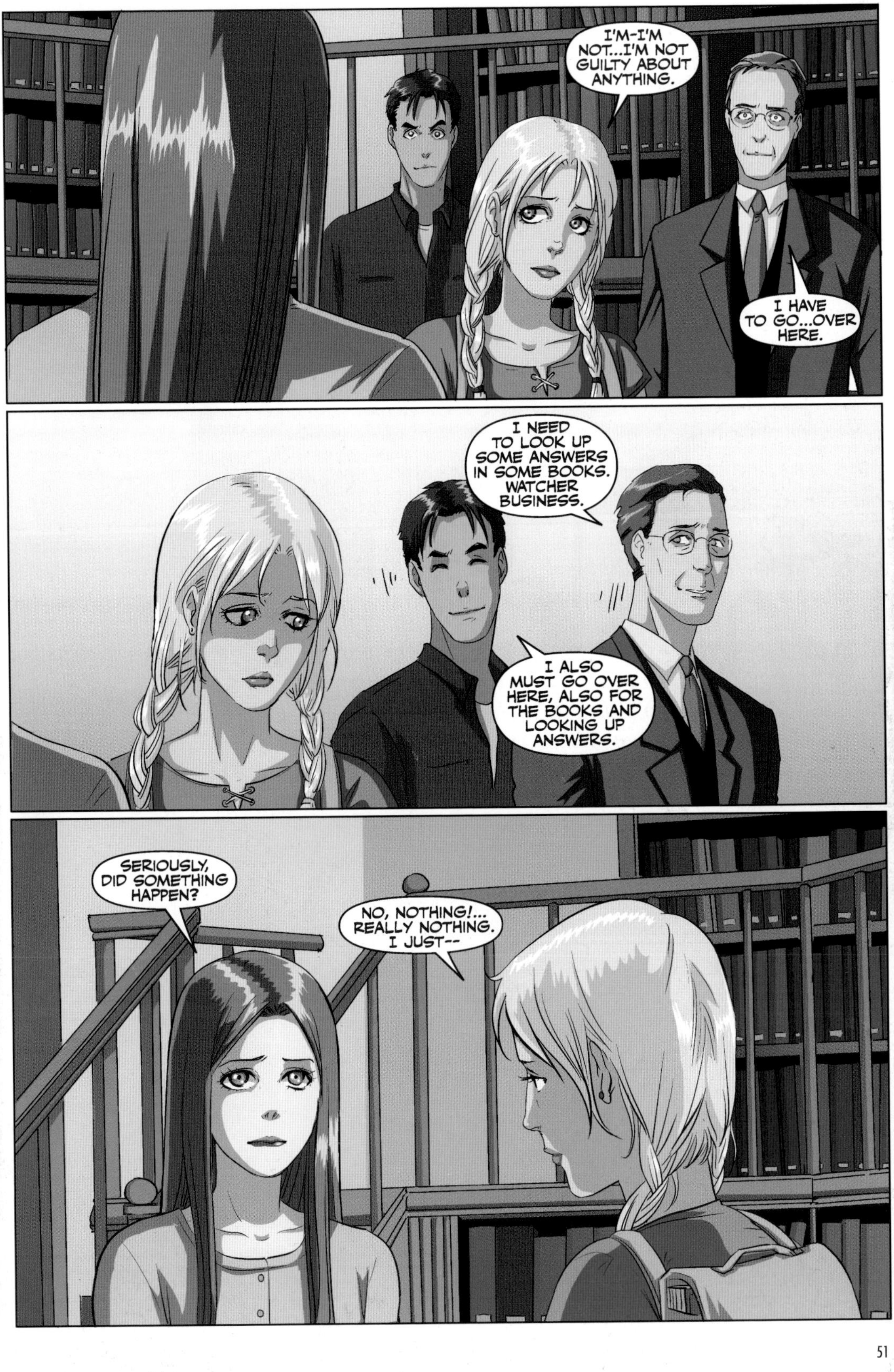
I'M-I'M NOT...I'M NOT GUILTY ABOUT ANYTHING.
I HAVE TO GO...OVER HERE.
I NEED TO LOOK UP SOME ANSWERS IN SOME BOOKS. WATCHER BUSINESS.
I ALSO MUST GO OVER HERE, ALSO FOR THE BOOKS AND LOOKING UP ANSWERS.
SERIOUSLY, DID SOMETHING HAPPEN?
NO, NOTHING!... REALLY NOTHING. I JUST--

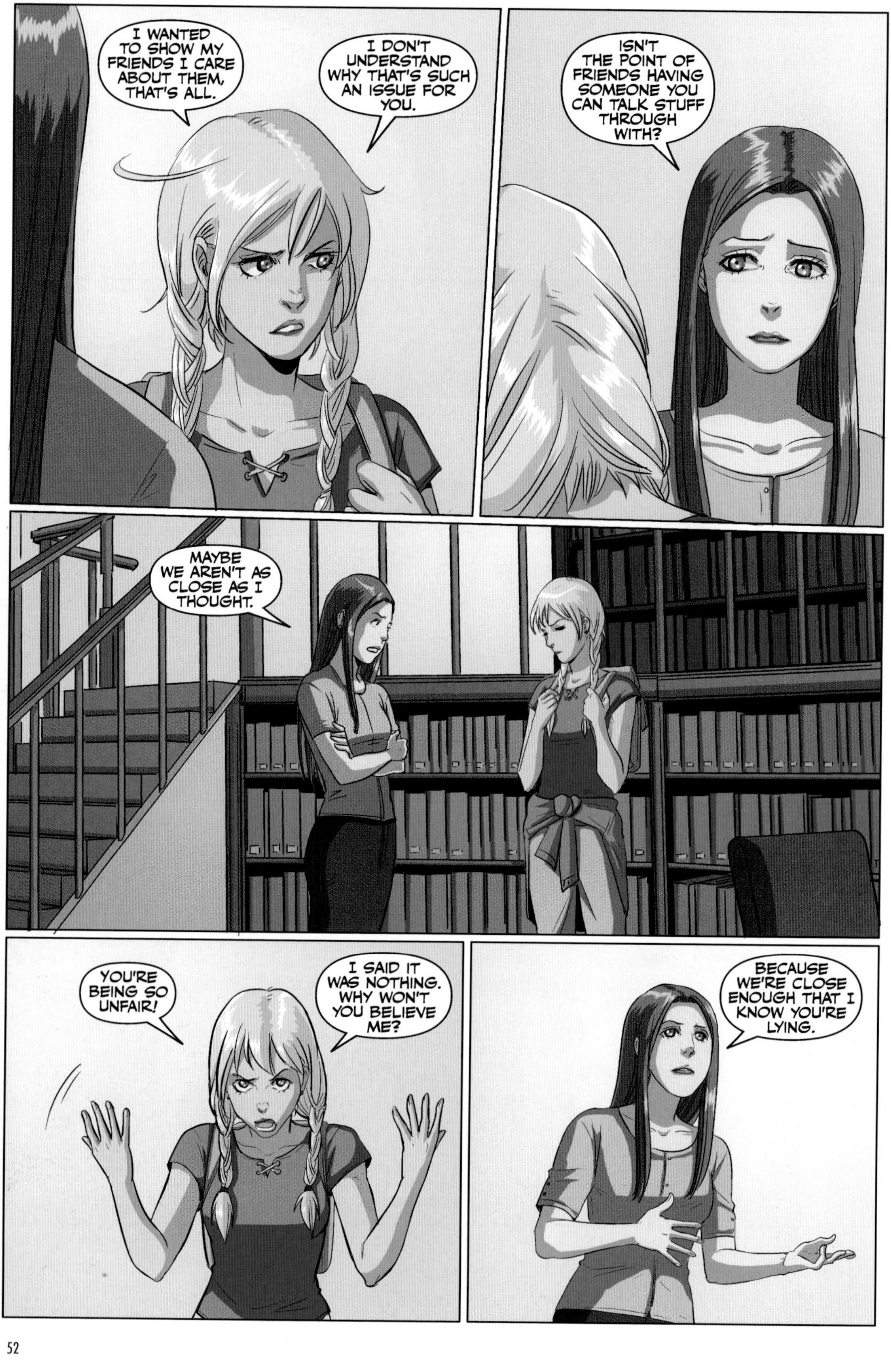
I WANTED TO SHOW MY FRIENDS I CARE ABOUT THEM, THAT'S ALL.
I DON'T UNDERSTAND WHY THAT'S SUCH AN ISSUE FOR YOU.
ISN'T THE POINT OF FRIENDS HAVING SOMEONE YOU CAN TALK STUFF THROUGH WITH?
MAYBE WE AREN'T AS CLOSE AS I THOUGHT.
YOU'RE BEING SO UNFAIR!
I SAID IT WAS NOTHING. WHY WON'T YOU BELIEVE ME?
BECAUSE WE'RE CLOSE ENOUGH THAT I KNOW YOU'RE LYING.

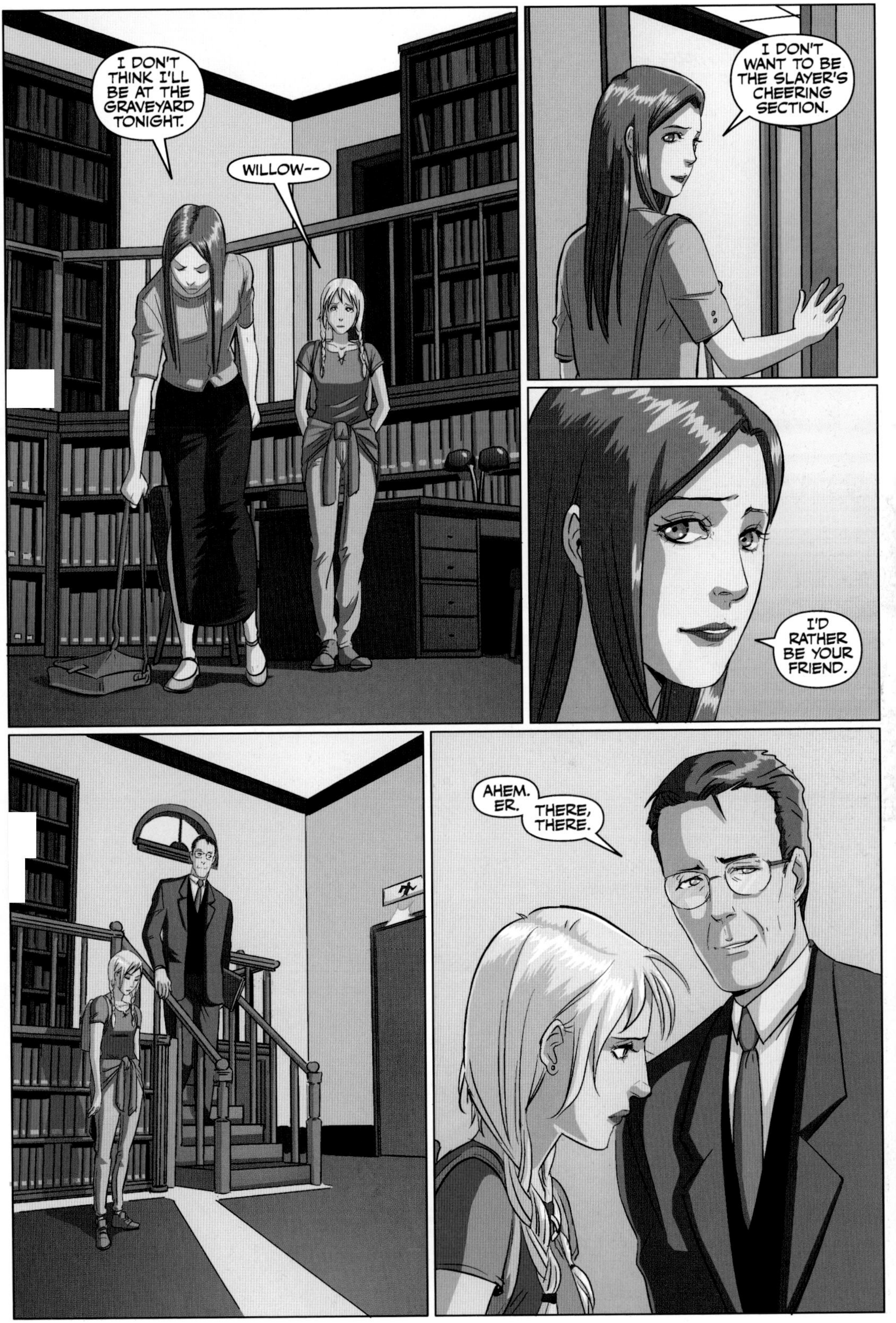
I DON'T THINK I'LL BE AT THE GRAVEYARD TONIGHT.
WILLOW--
I DON'T WANT TO BE THE SLAYER'S CHEERING SECTION.
I'D RATHER BE YOUR FRIEND.
AHEM. ER.
THERE, THERE.

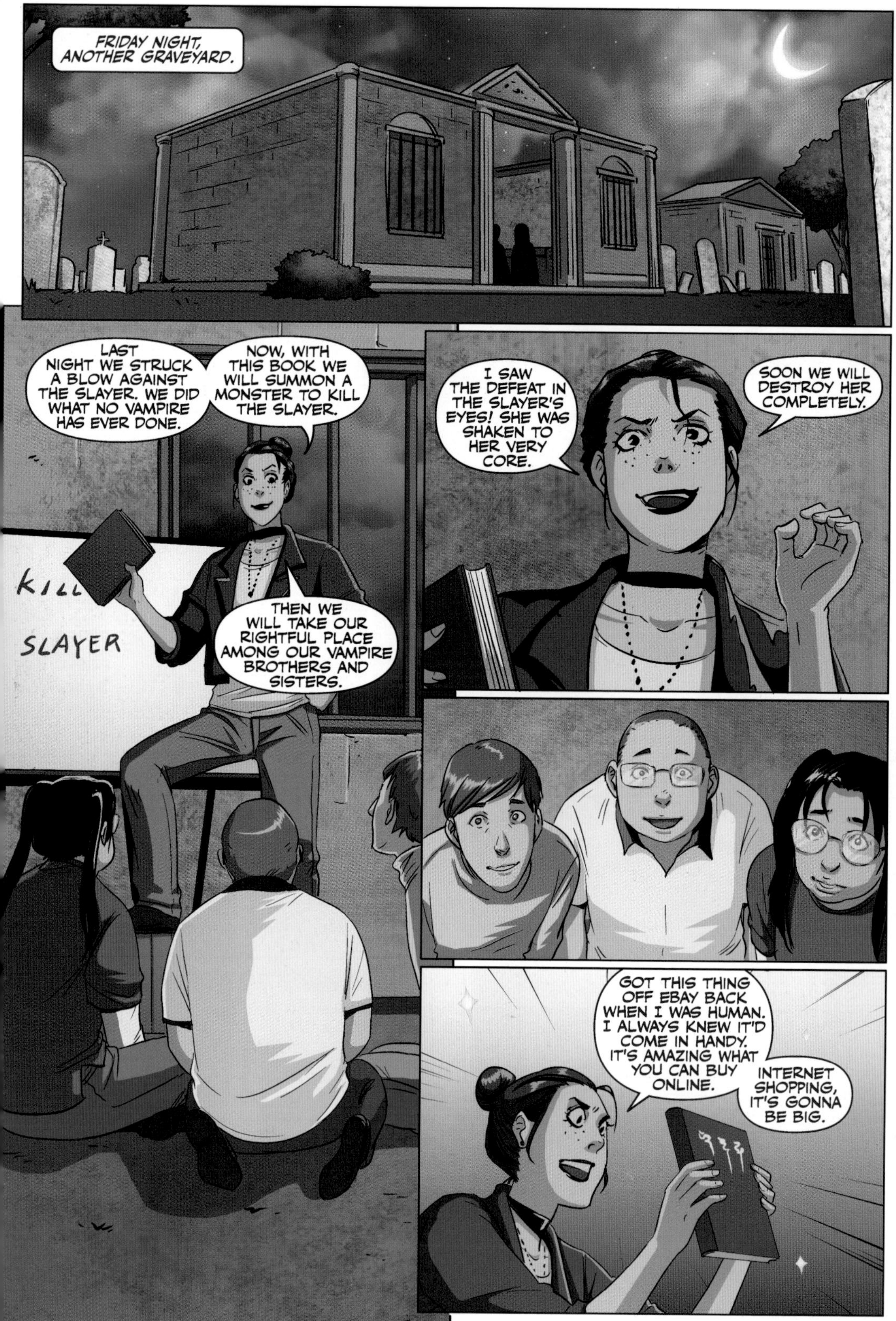
FRIDAY NIGHT, ANOTHER GRAVEYARD.
LAST NIGHT WE STRUCK A BLOW AGAINST THE SLAYER. WE DID WHAT NO VAMPIRE HAS EVER DONE.
NOW, WITH THIS BOOK WE WILL SUMMON A MONSTER TO KILL THE SLAYER.
THEN WE WILL TAKE OUR RIGHTFUL PLACE AMONG OUR VAMPIRE BROTHERS AND SISTERS.
SLAYER
I SAW THE DEFEAT IN THE SLAYER'S EYES! SHE WAS SHAKEN TO HER VERY CORE.
SOON WE WILL DESTROY HER COMPLETELY.
GOT THIS THING OFF EBAY BACK WHEN I WAS HUMAN. I ALWAYS KNEW IT'D COME IN HANDY. IT'S AMAZING WHAT YOU CAN BUY ONLINE.
INTERNET SHOPPING, IT'S GONNA BE BIG.

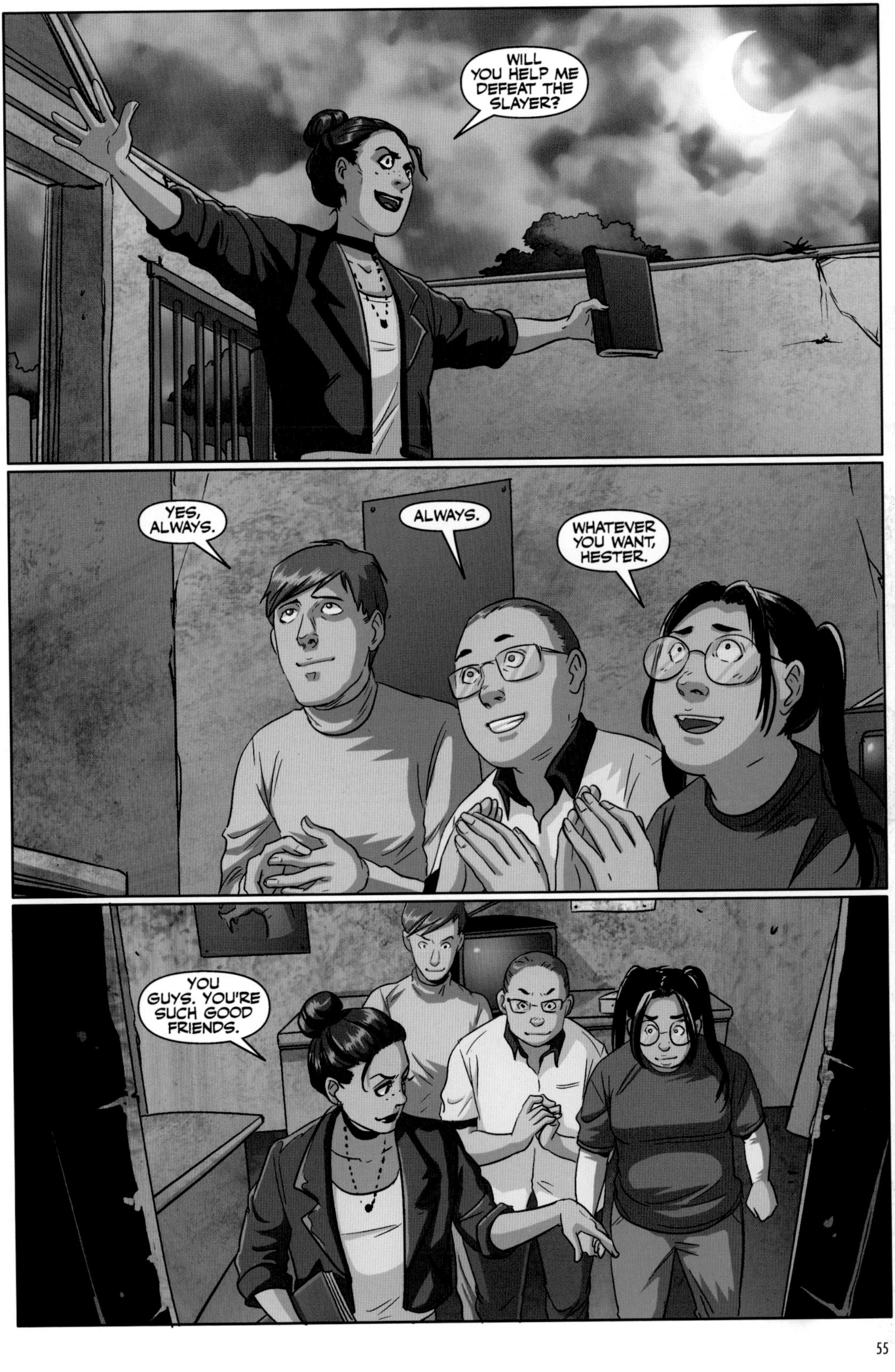

WILL YOU HELP ME DEFEAT THE SLAYER?
YES, ALWAYS.
ALWAYS.
WHATEVER YOU WANT, HESTER.
YOU GUYS. YOU'RE SUCH GOOD FRIENDS.

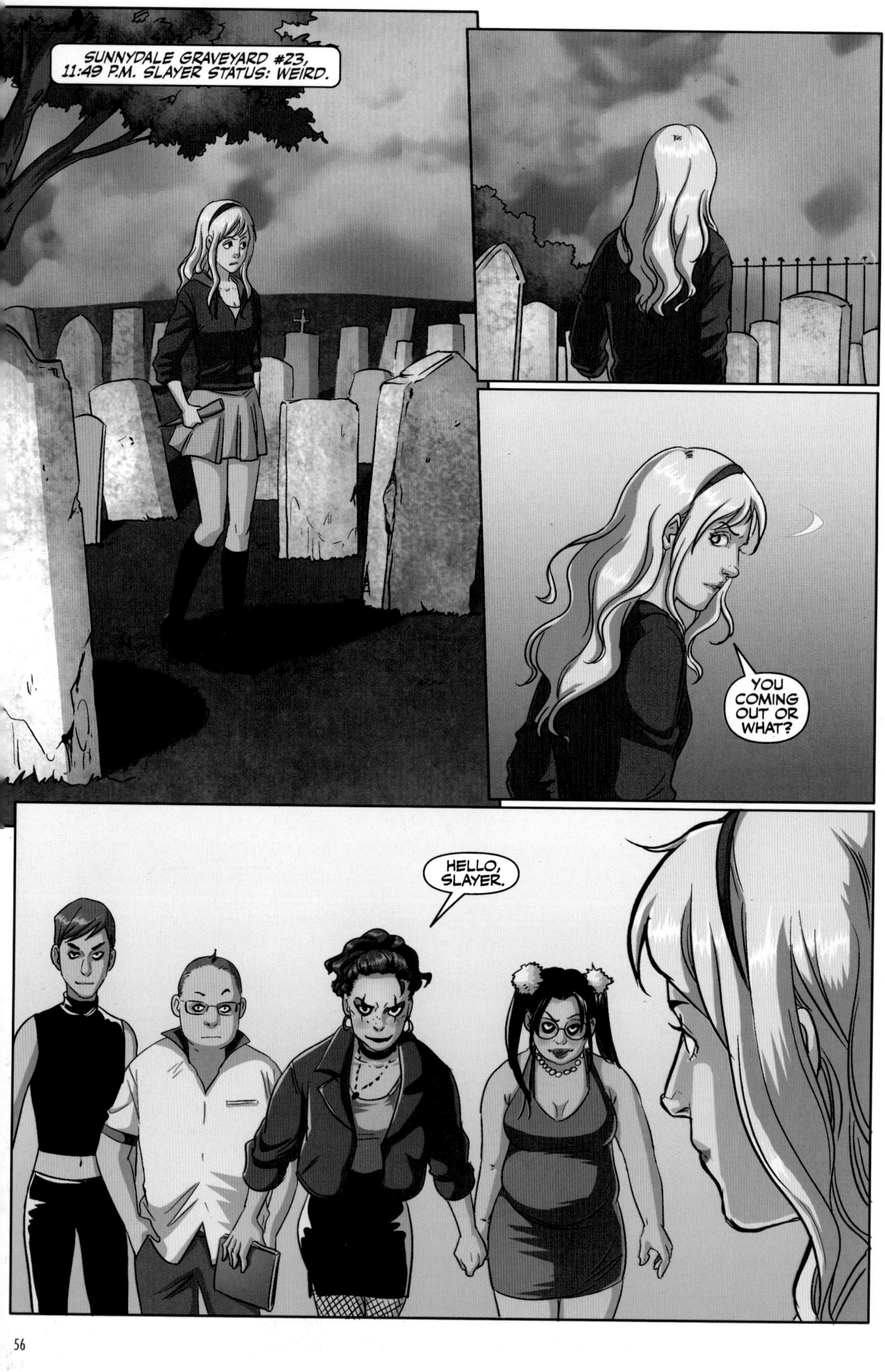
SUNNYDALE GRAVEYARD #23, 11:49 P.M. SLAYER STATUS: WEIRD.
YOU COMING OUT OR WHAT?
HELLO, SLAYER.

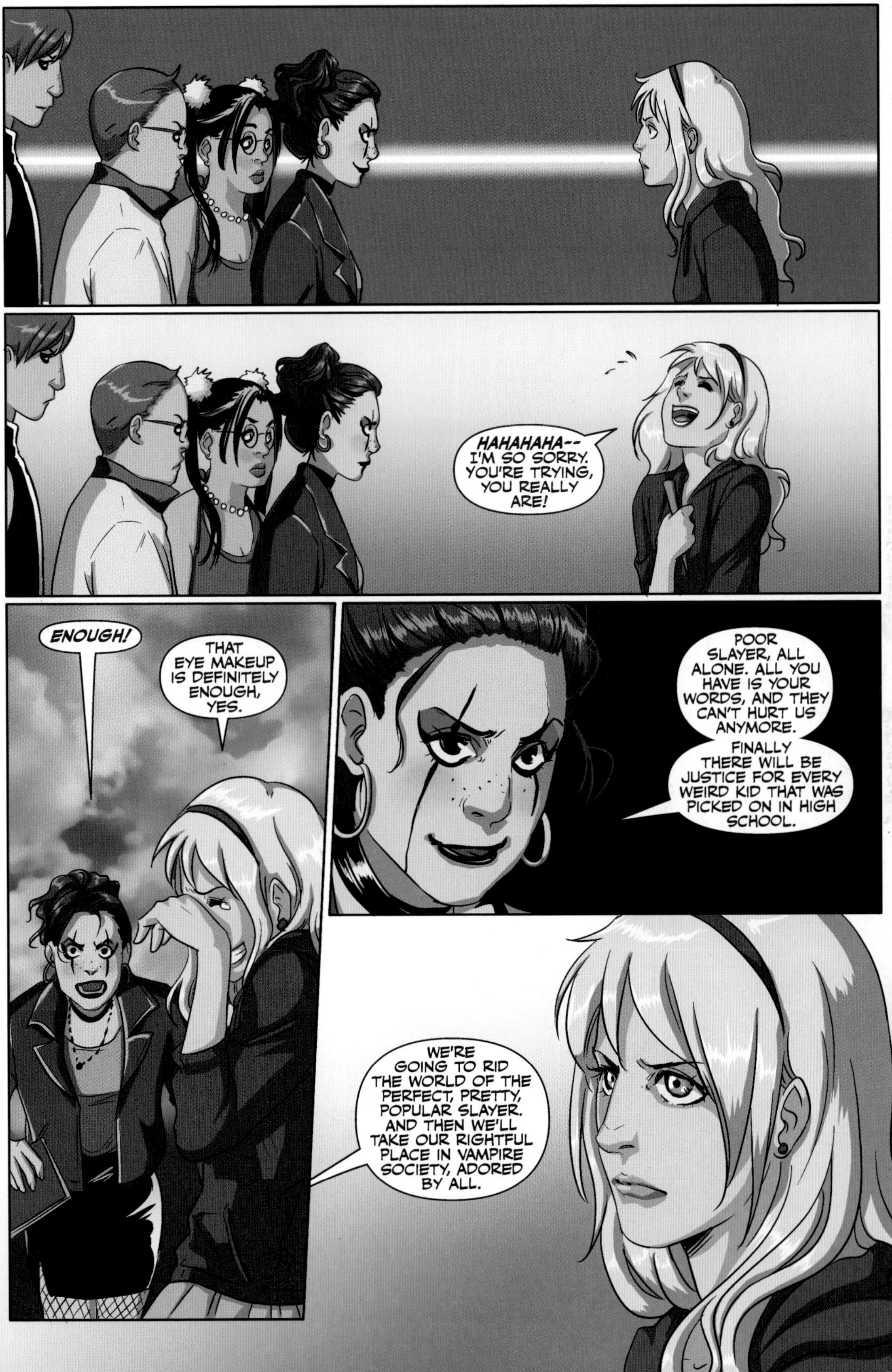
HAHAHAHA-- I'M SO SORRY. YOU'RE TRYING, YOU REALLY ARE!
ENOUGH!
THAT EYE MAKEUP IS DEFINITELY ENOUGH, YES.
POOR SLAYER, ALL ALONE. ALL YOU HAVE IS YOUR WORDS, AND THEY CAN'T HURT US ANYMORE.
FINALLY THERE WILL BE JUSTICE FOR EVERY WEIRD KID THAT WAS PICKED ON IN HIGH SCHOOL.
WE'RE GOING TO RID THE WORLD OF THE PERFECT, PRETTY, POPULAR SLAYER. AND THEN WE'LL TAKE OUR RIGHTFUL PLACE IN VAMPIRE SOCIETY, ADORED BY ALL.

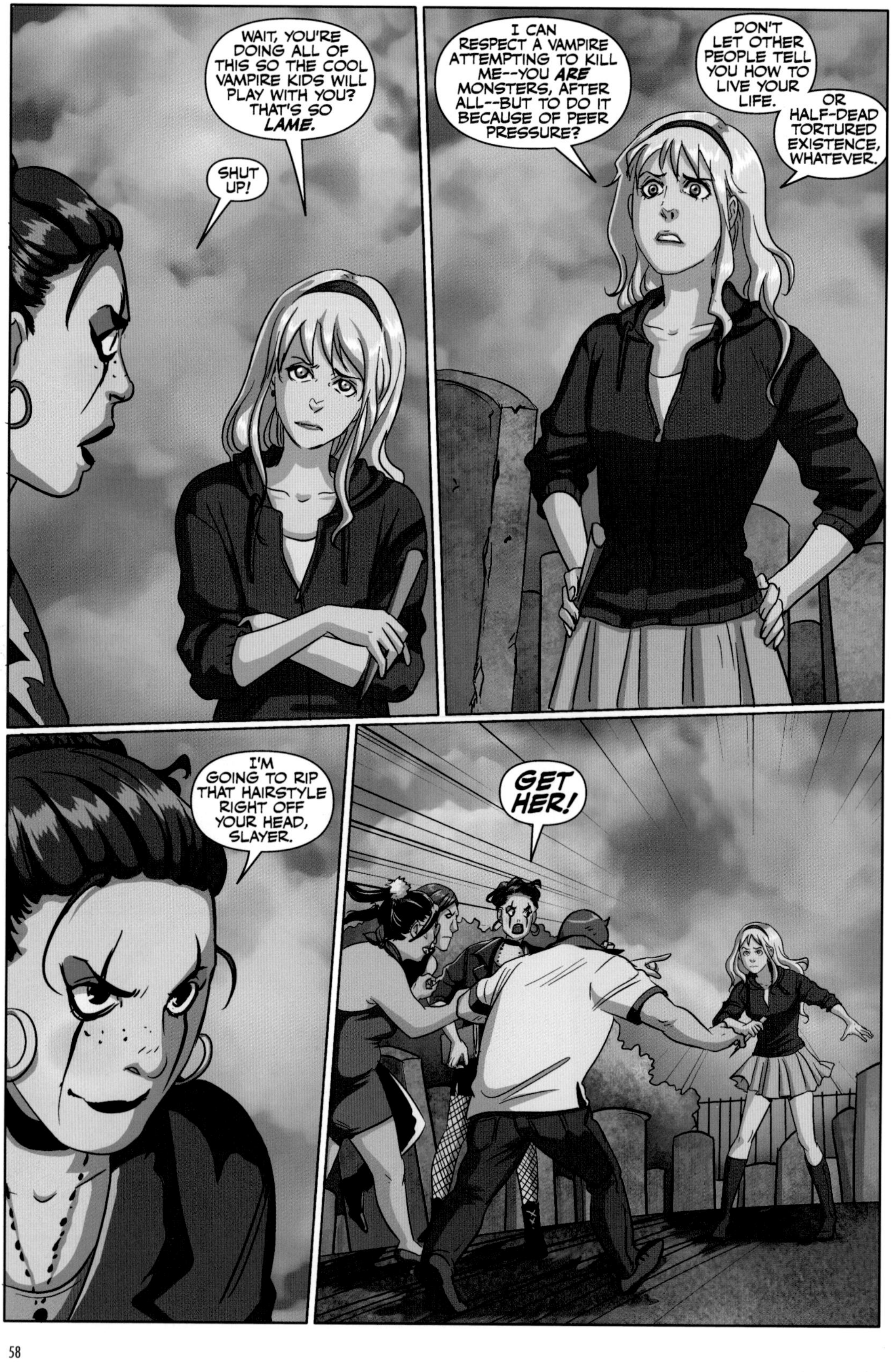
WAIT, YOU'RE DOING ALL OF THIS SO THE COOL VAMPIRE KIDS WILL PLAY WITH YOU? THAT'S SO LAME.
SHUT UP!
I CAN RESPECT A VAMPIRE ATTEMPTING TO KILL ME--YOU ARE MONSTERS, AFTER ALL--BUT TO DO IT BECAUSE OF PEER PRESSURE?
DON'T LET OTHER PEOPLE TELL YOU HOW TO LIVE YOUR LIFE.
OR HALF-DEAD TORTURED EXISTENCE, WHATEVER.
I'M GOING TO RIP THAT HAIRSTYLE RIGHT OFF YOUR HEAD, SLAYER.
GET HER!

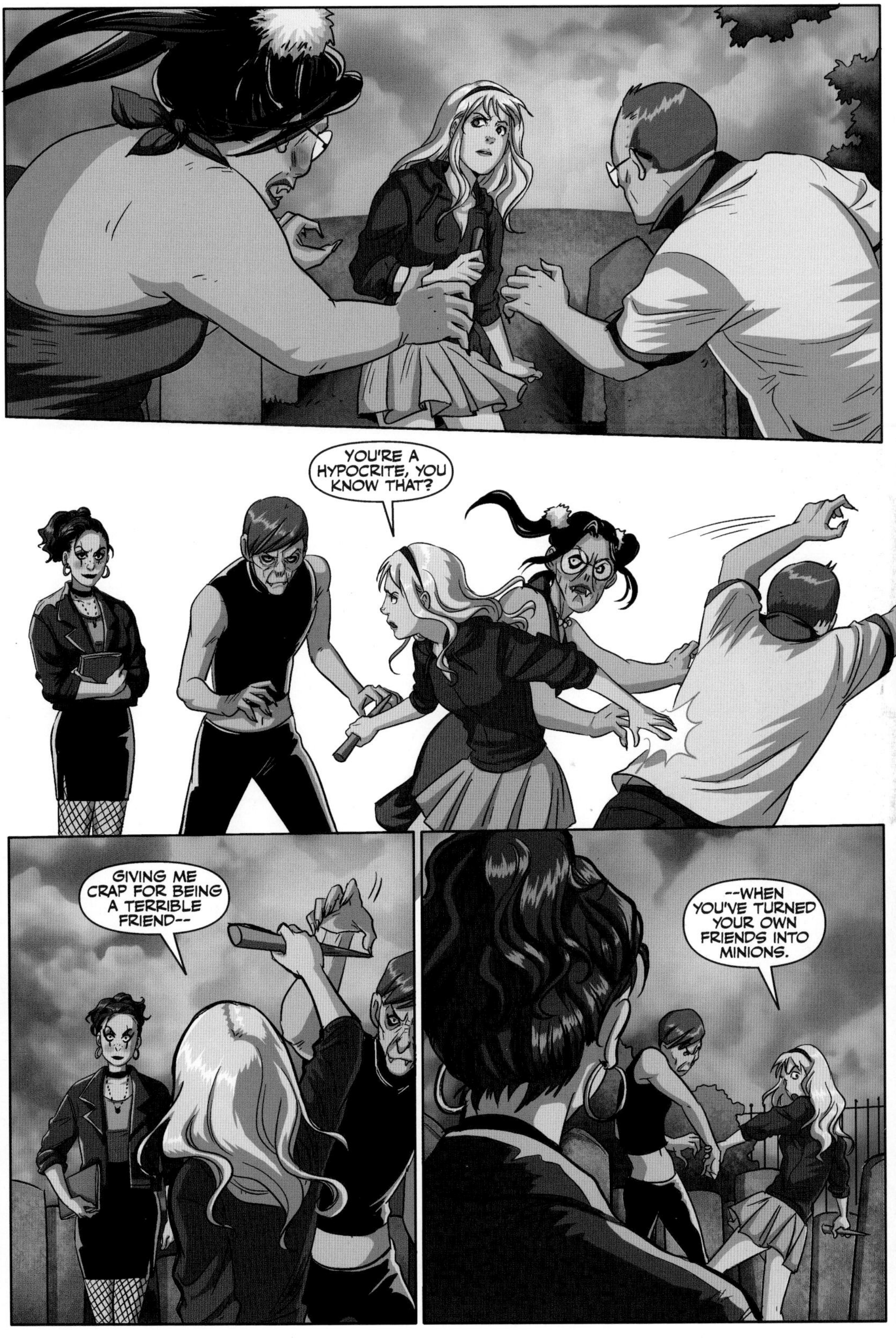
YOU'RE A HYPOCRITE, YOU KNOW THAT?
GIVING ME CRAP FOR BEING A TERRIBLE FRIEND--
--WHEN YOU'VE TURNED YOUR OWN FRIENDS INTO MINIONS.

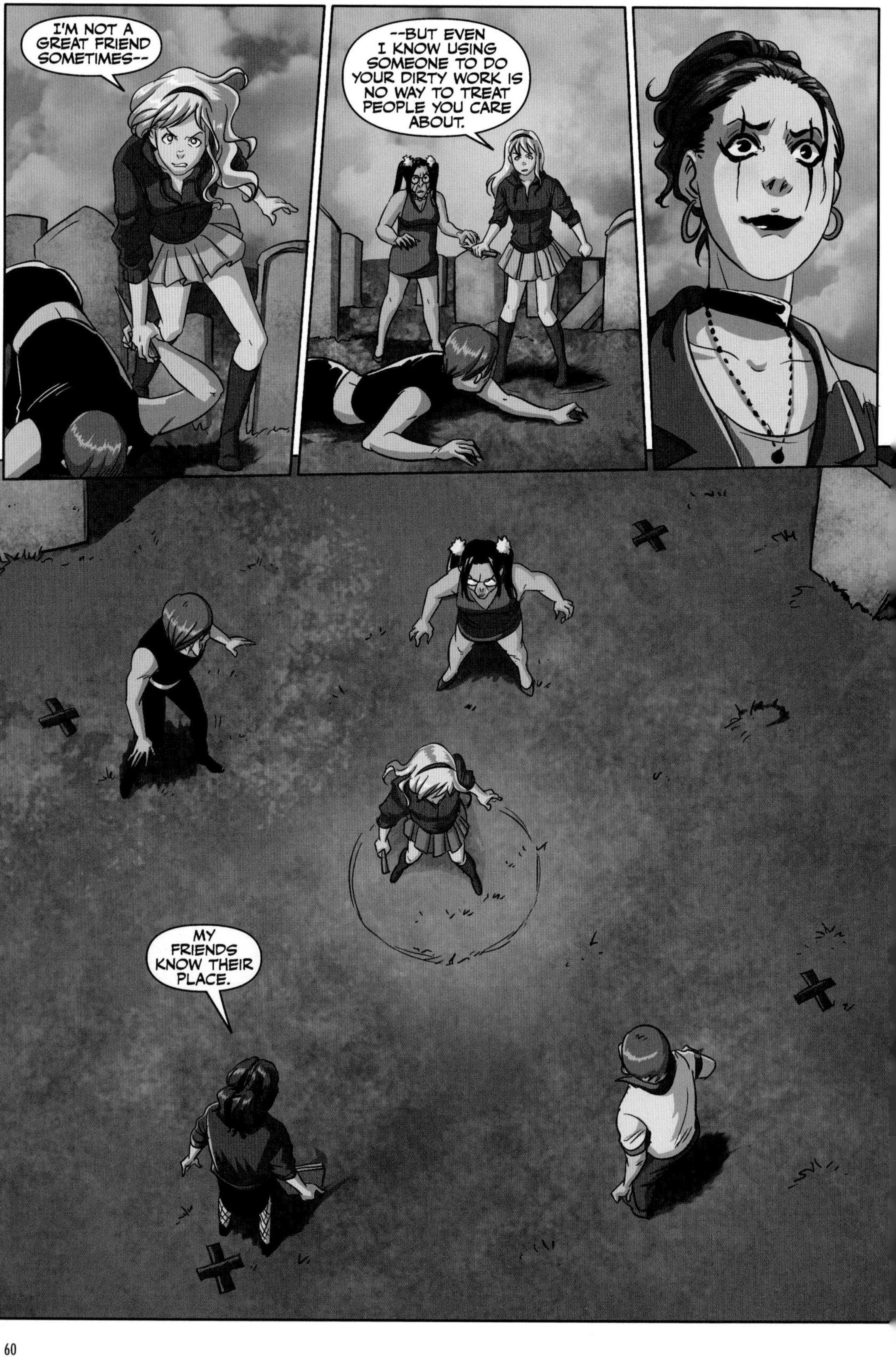
I'M NOT A GREAT FRIEND SOMETIMES--
--BUT EVEN I KNOW USING SOMEONE TO DO YOUR DIRTY WORK IS NO WAY TO TREAT PEOPLE YOU CARE ABOUT.
MY FRIENDS KNOW THEIR PLACE.

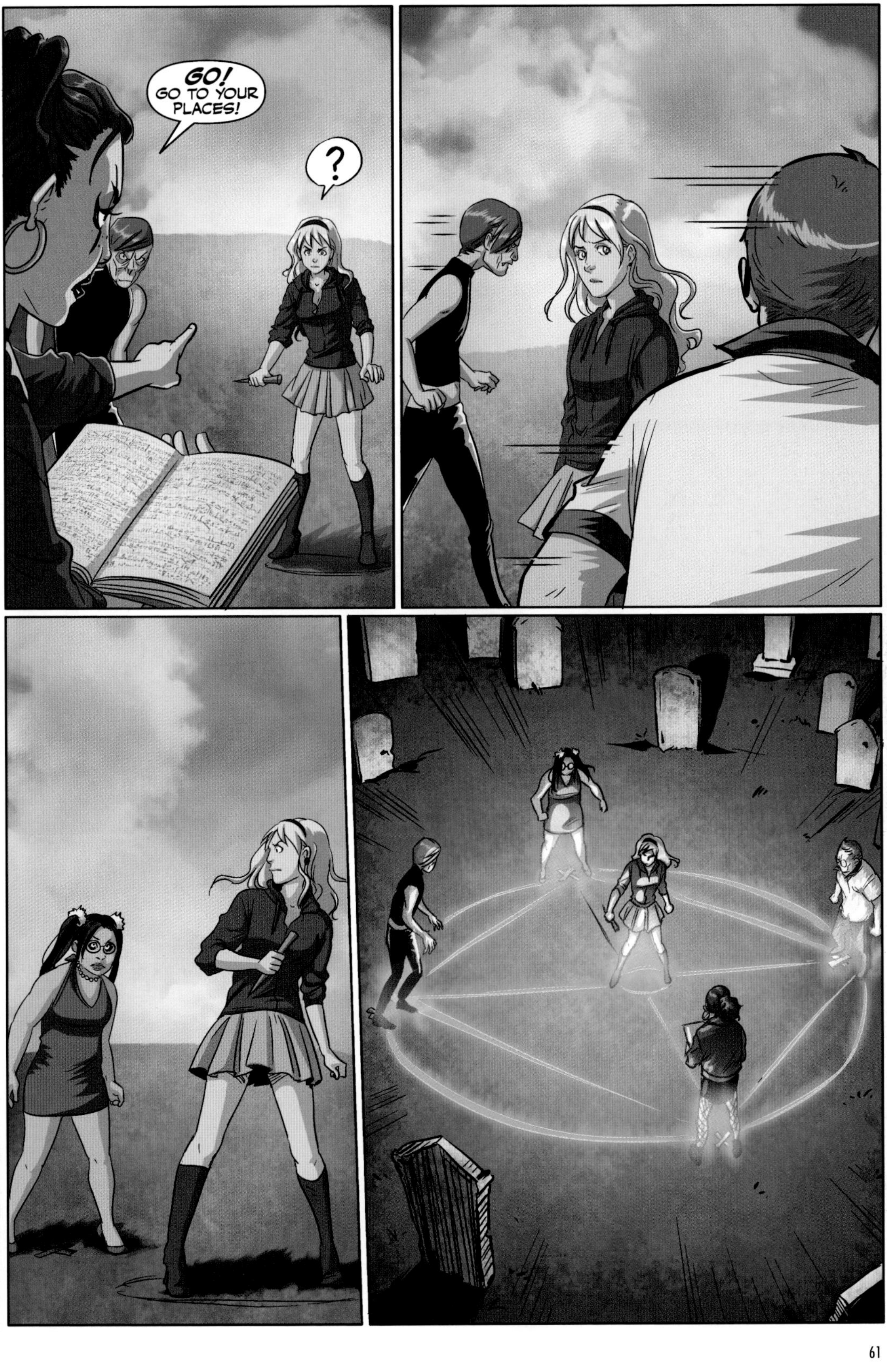
GO! GO TO YOUR PLACES!
?

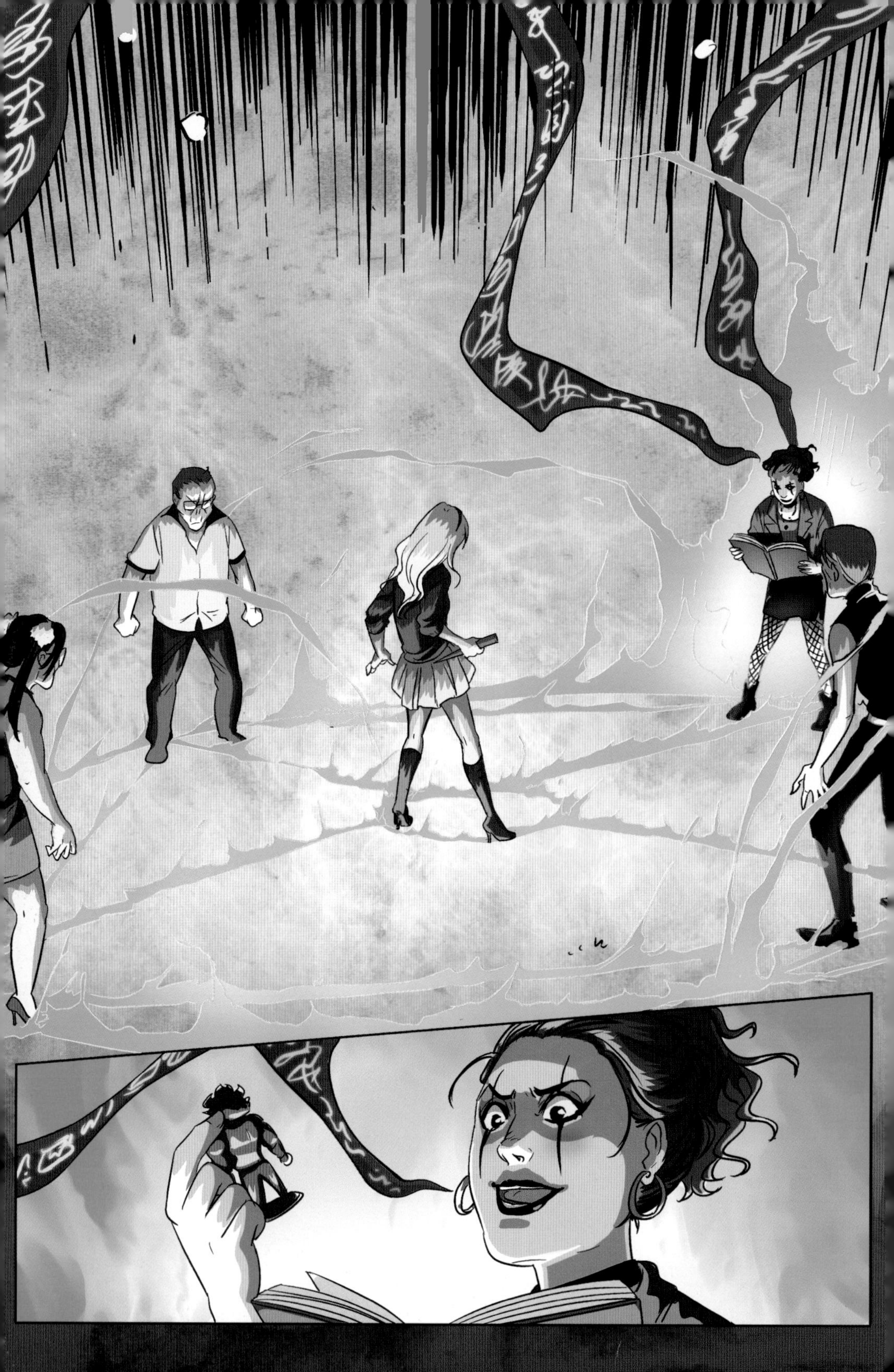

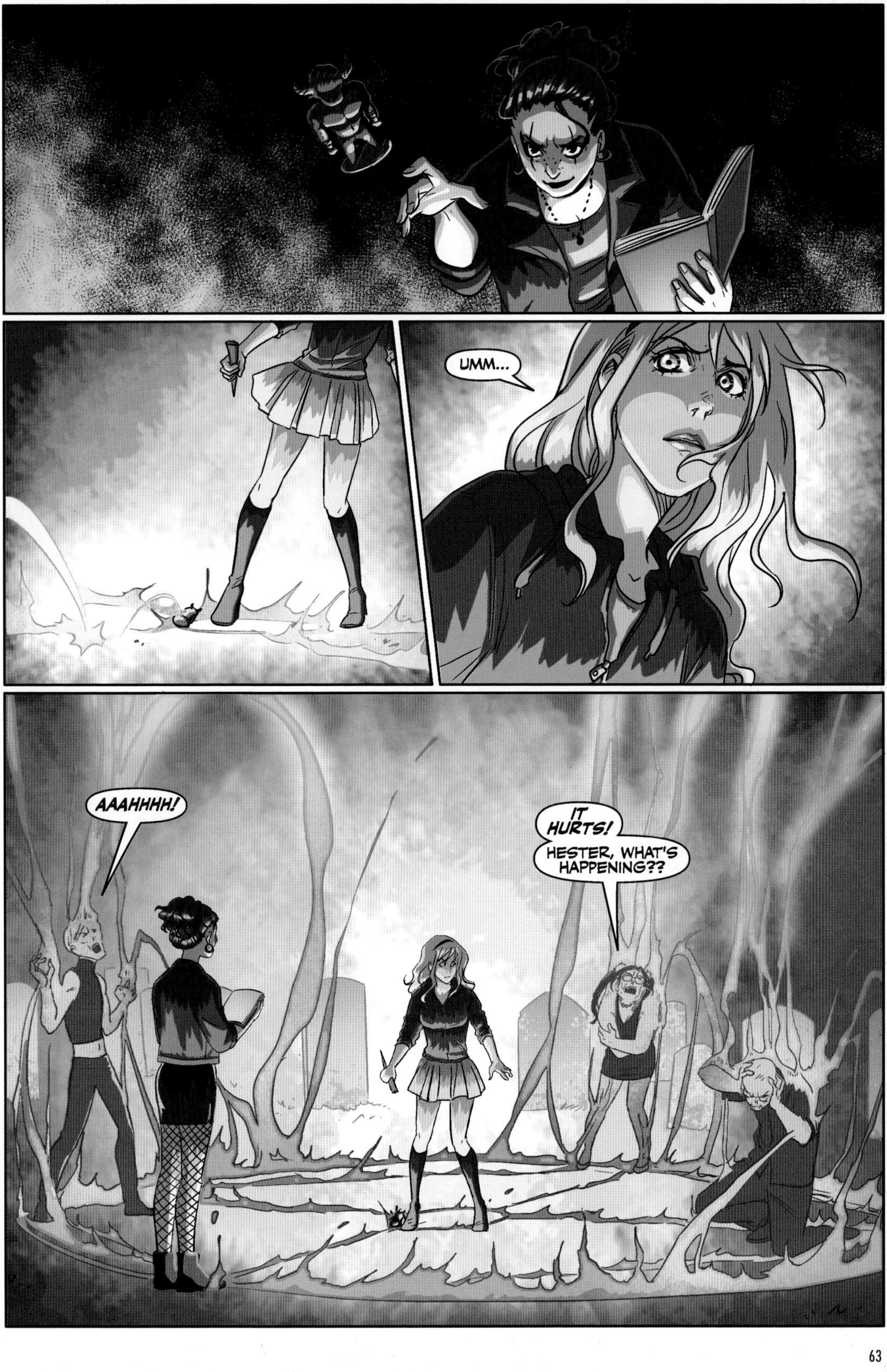
UMM...
AAAHHHH!
IT HURTS!
HESTER, WHAT'S HAPPENING??

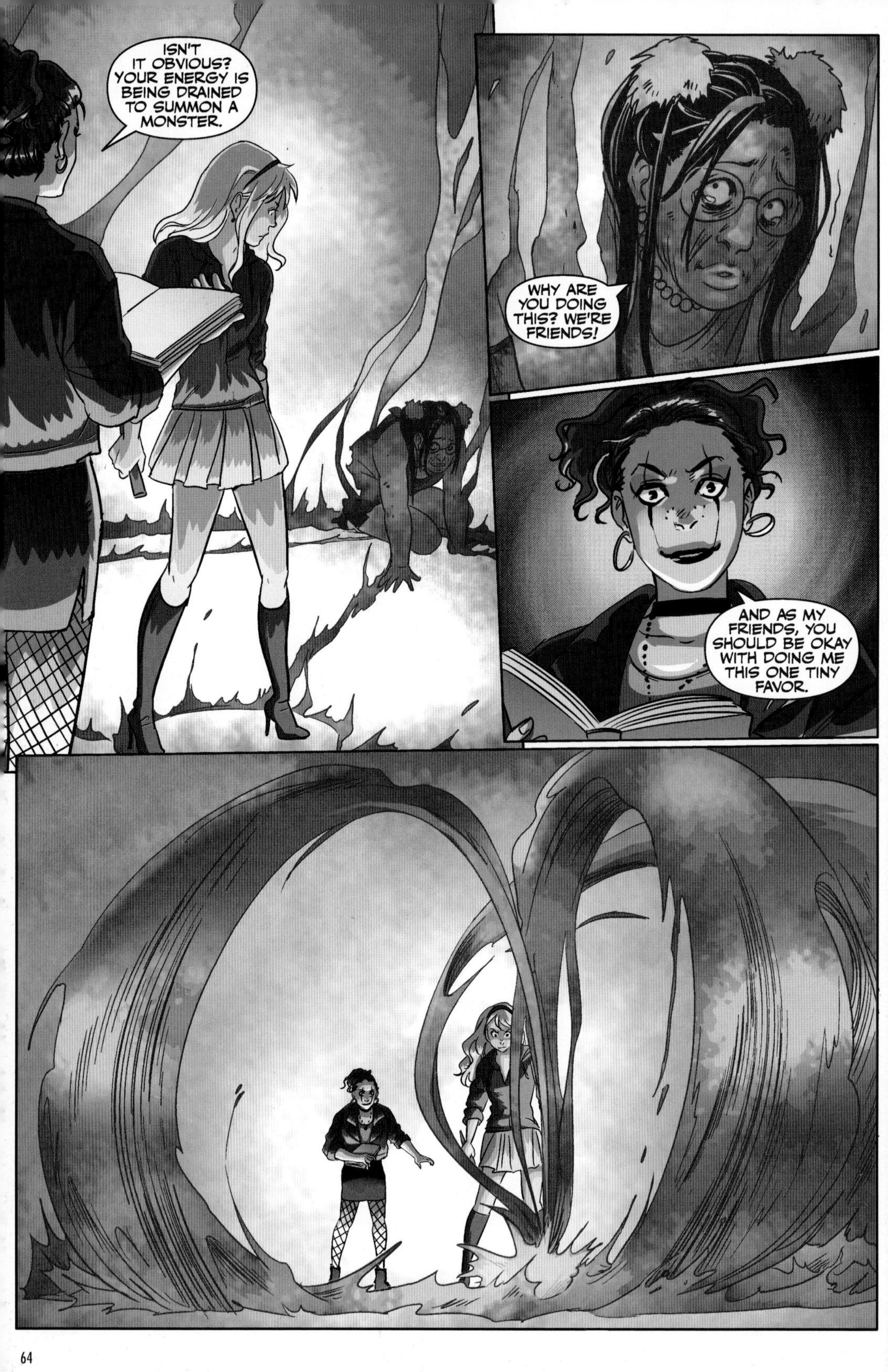

ISN'T IT OBVIOUS? YOUR ENERGY IS BEING DRAINED TO SUMMON A MONSTER.
WHY ARE YOU DOING THIS? WE'RE FRIENDS!
AND AS MY FRIENDS, YOU SHOULD BE OKAY WITH DOING ME THIS ONE TINY FAVOR.

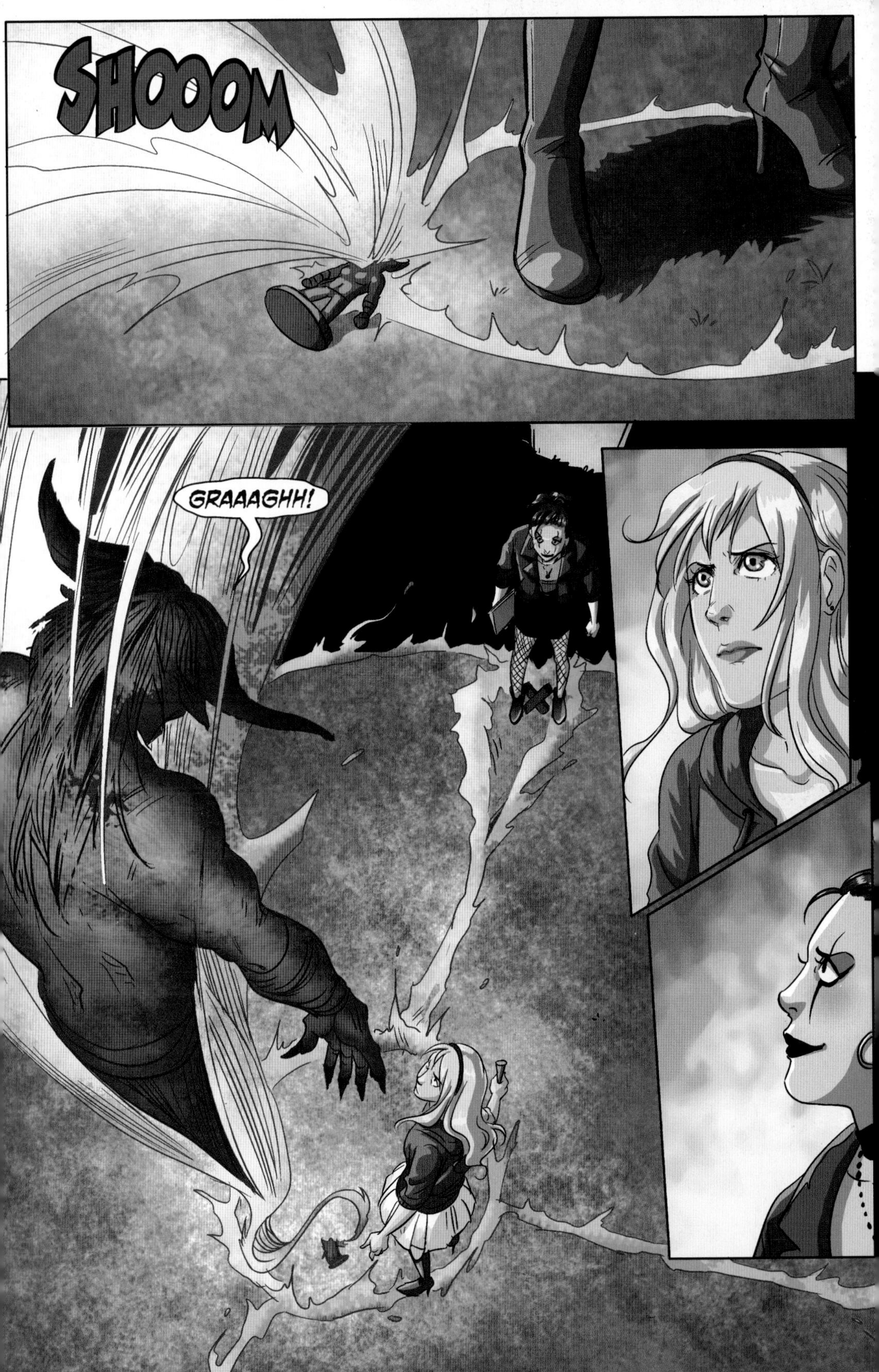
SHOOOM
GRAAAGHH!

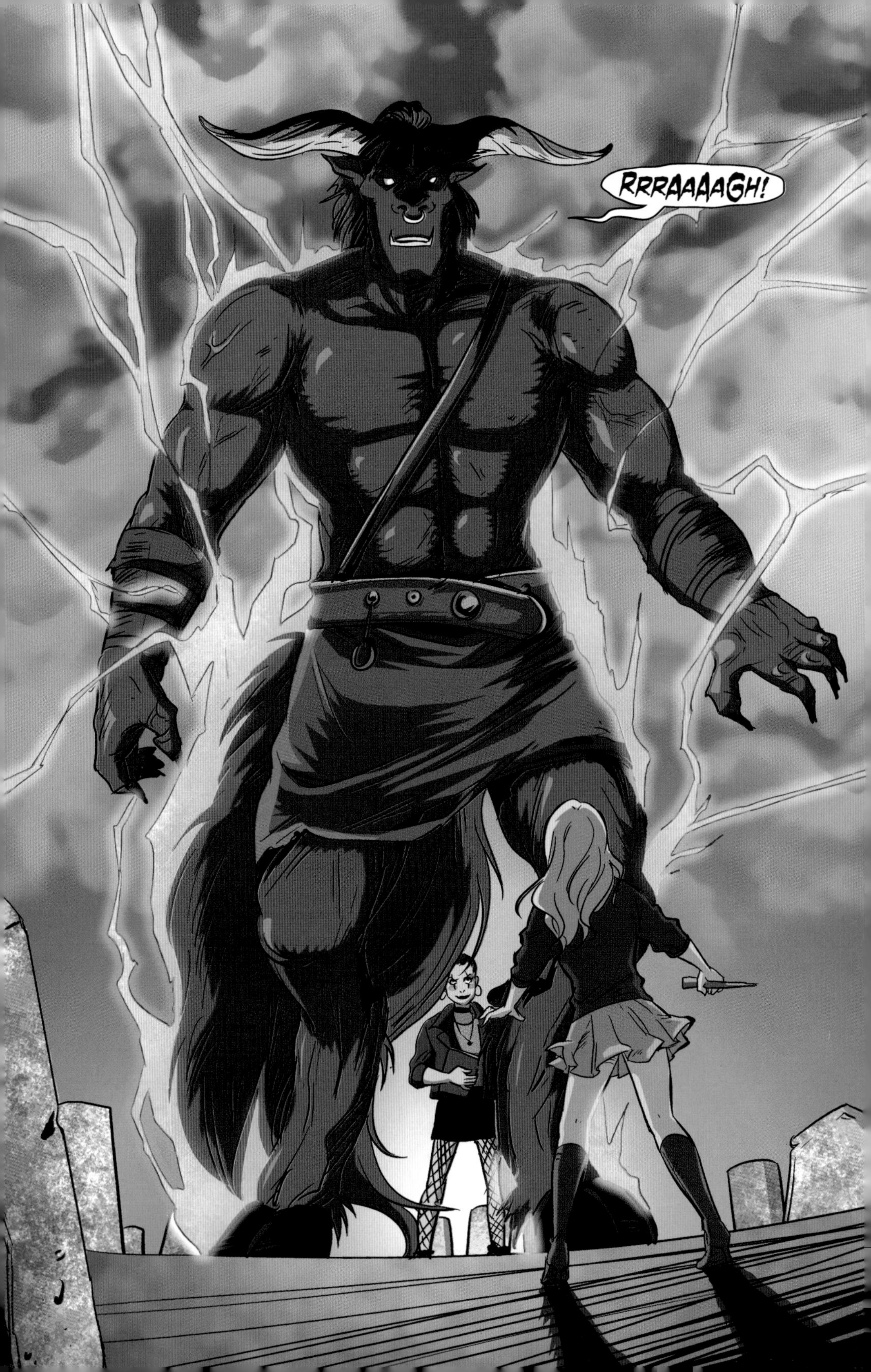
RRRAAAAAGH!

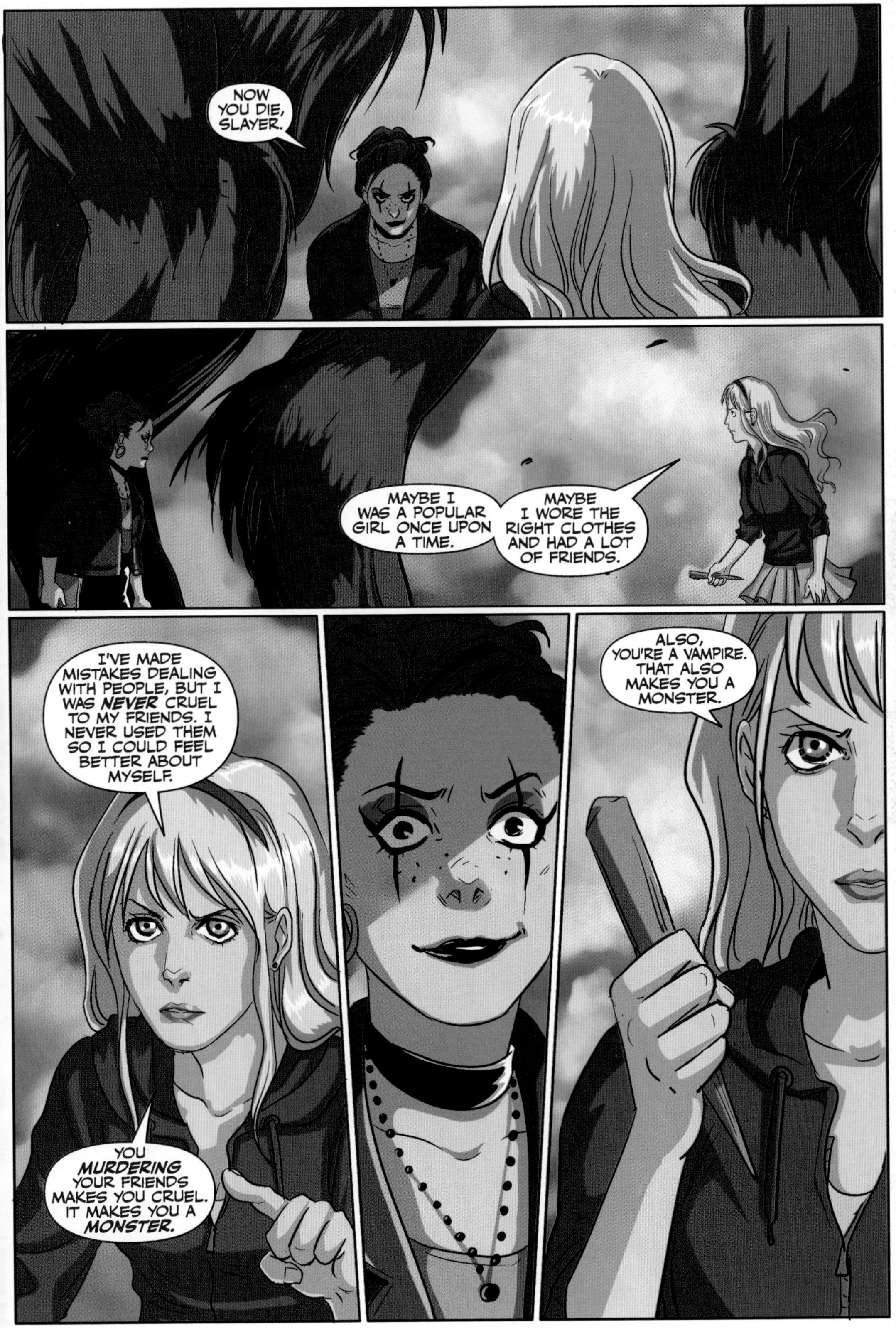
NOW YOU DIE, SLAYER.
MAYBE I WAS A POPULAR GIRL ONCE UPON A TIME.
MAYBE I WORE THE RIGHT CLOTHES AND HAD A LOT OF FRIENDS.
I'VE MADE MISTAKES DEALING WITH PEOPLE, BUT I WAS *NEVER* CRUEL TO MY FRIENDS. I NEVER USED THEM SO I COULD FEEL BETTER ABOUT MYSELF.
YOU *MURDERING* YOUR FRIENDS MAKES YOU CRUEL. IT MAKES YOU A *MONSTER.*
ALSO, YOU'RE A VAMPIRE. THAT ALSO MAKES YOU A MONSTER.

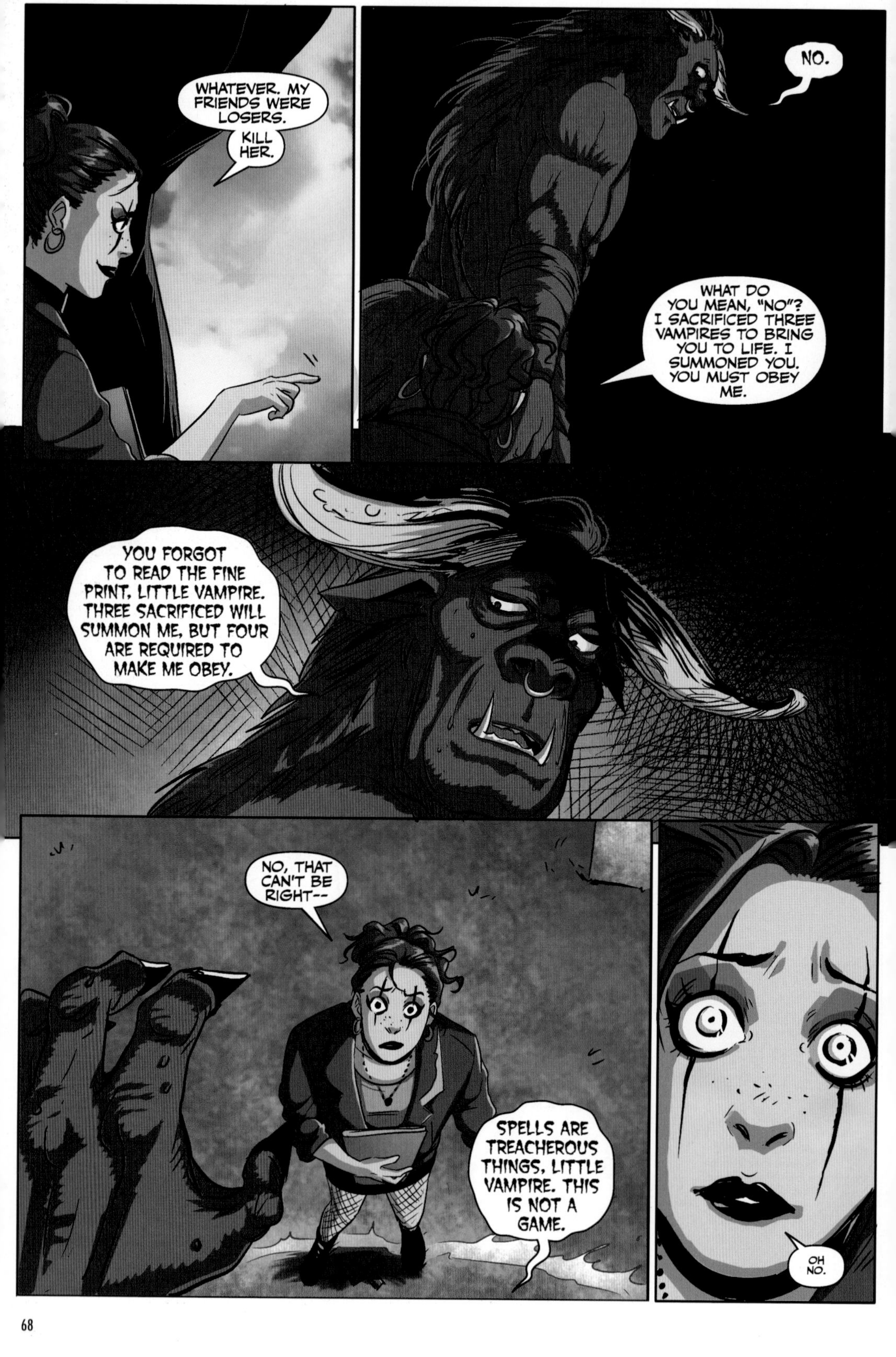
WHATEVER. MY FRIENDS WERE LOSERS.
KILL HER.
NO.
WHAT DO YOU MEAN, "NO"? I SACRIFICED THREE VAMPIRES TO BRING YOU TO LIFE. I SUMMONED YOU. YOU MUST OBEY ME.
YOU FORGOT TO READ THE FINE PRINT, LITTLE VAMPIRE. THREE SACRIFICED WILL SUMMON ME, BUT FOUR ARE REQUIRED TO MAKE ME OBEY.
NO, THAT CAN'T BE RIGHT--
SPELLS ARE TREACHEROUS THINGS, LITTLE VAMPIRE. THIS IS NOT A GAME.
OH NO.

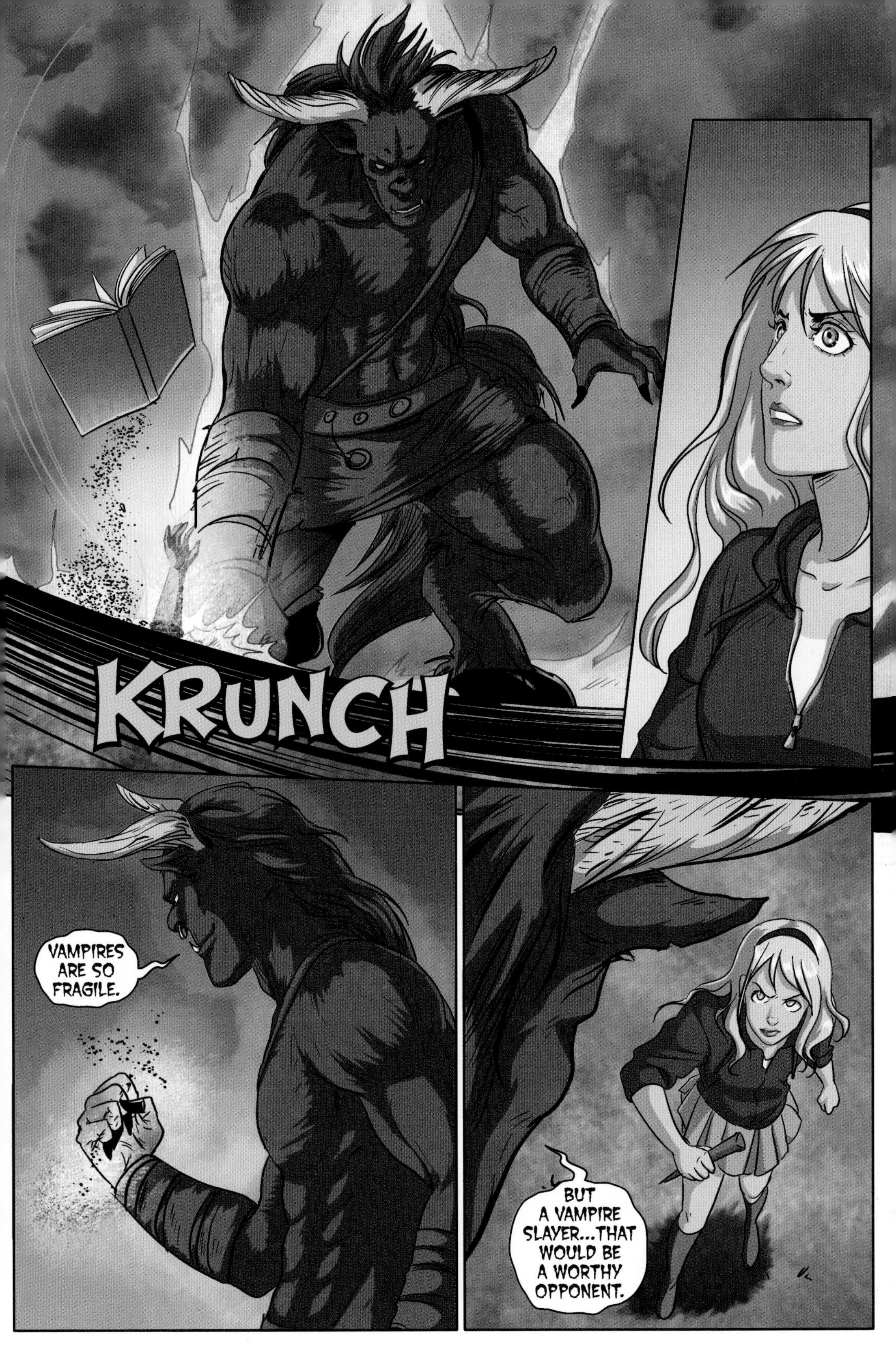
KRUNCH
VAMPIRES ARE SO FRAGILE.
BUT A VAMPIRE SLAYER...THAT WOULD BE A WORTHY OPPONENT.

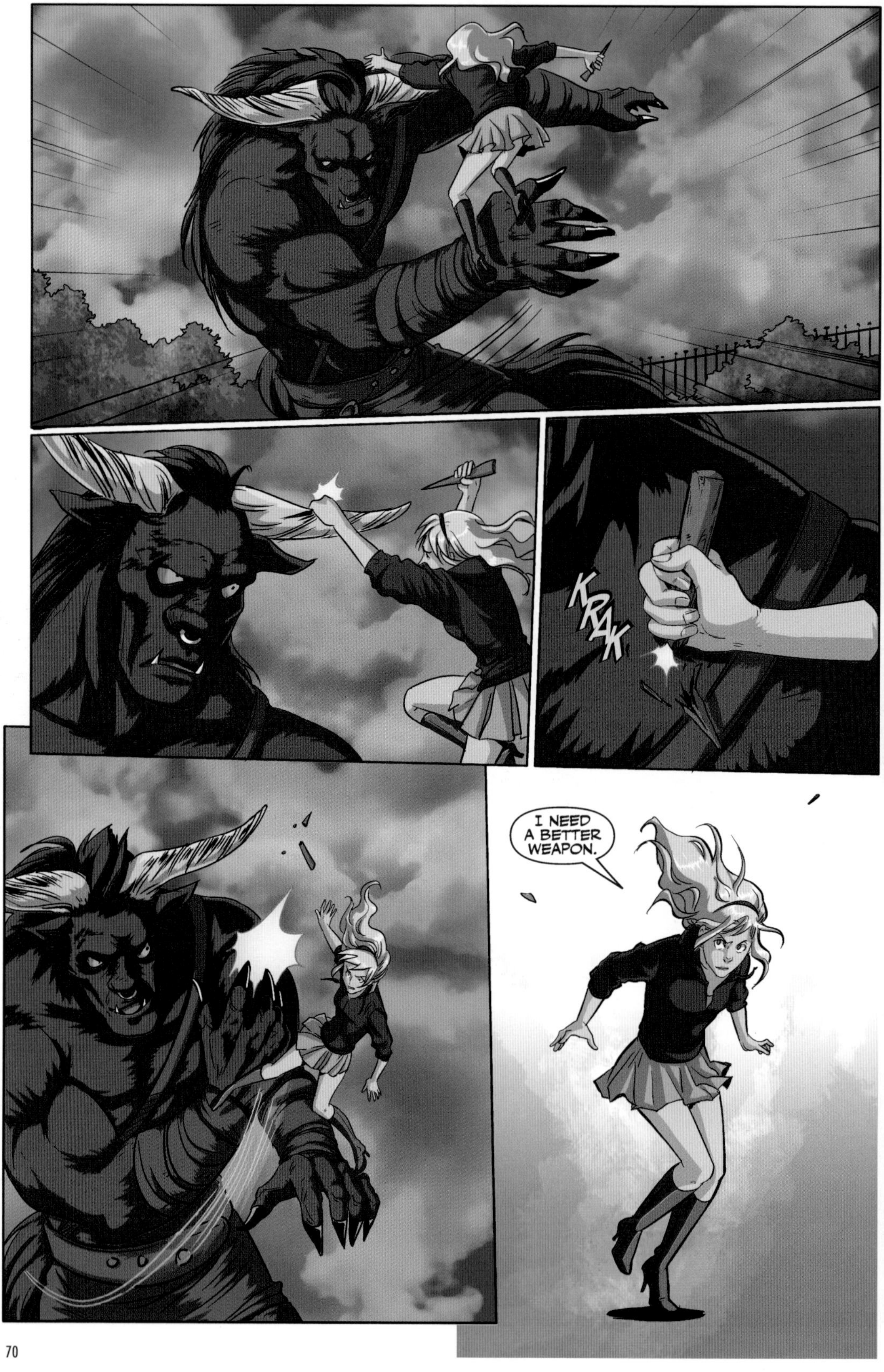
KRAK
I NEED A BETTER WEAPON.

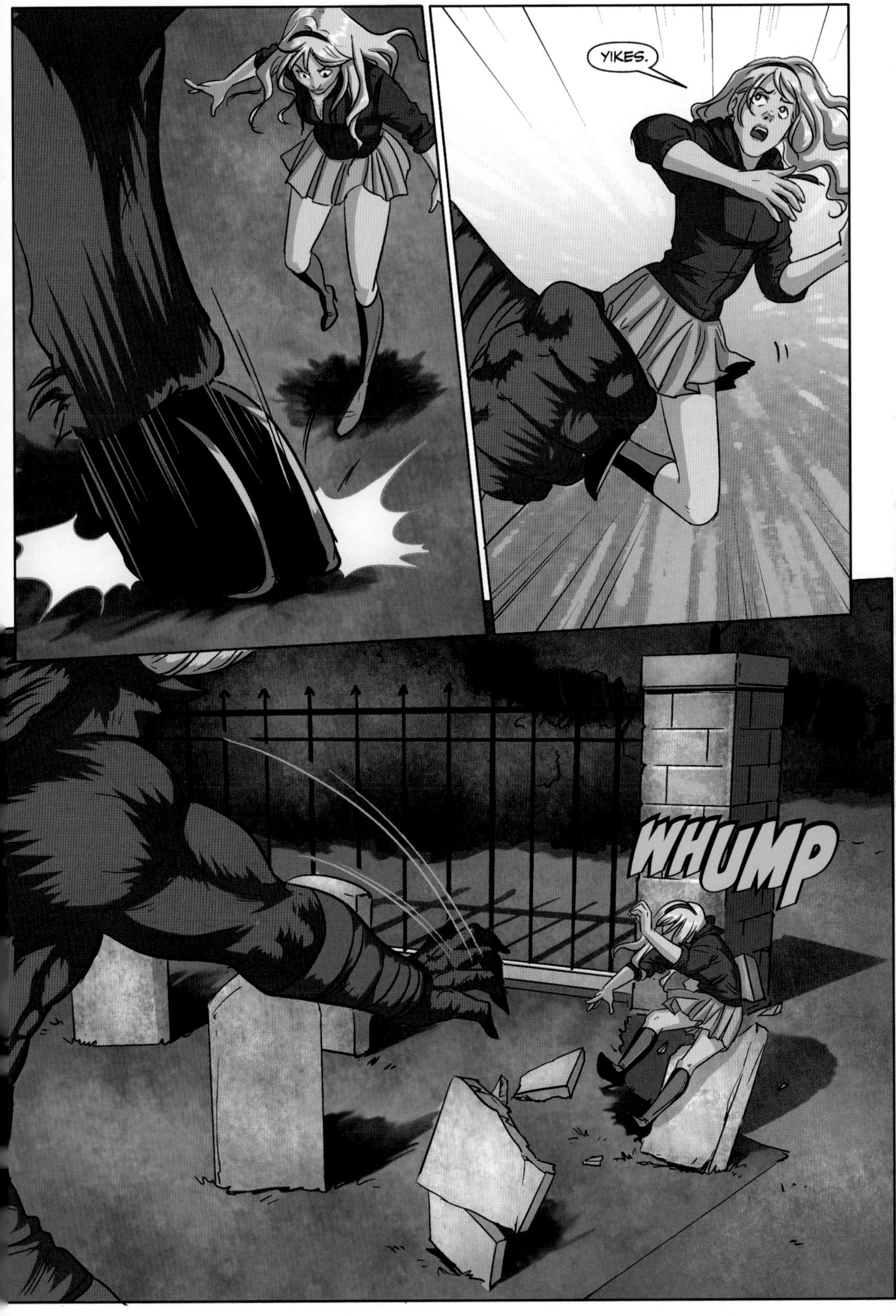
YIKES.
WHUMP

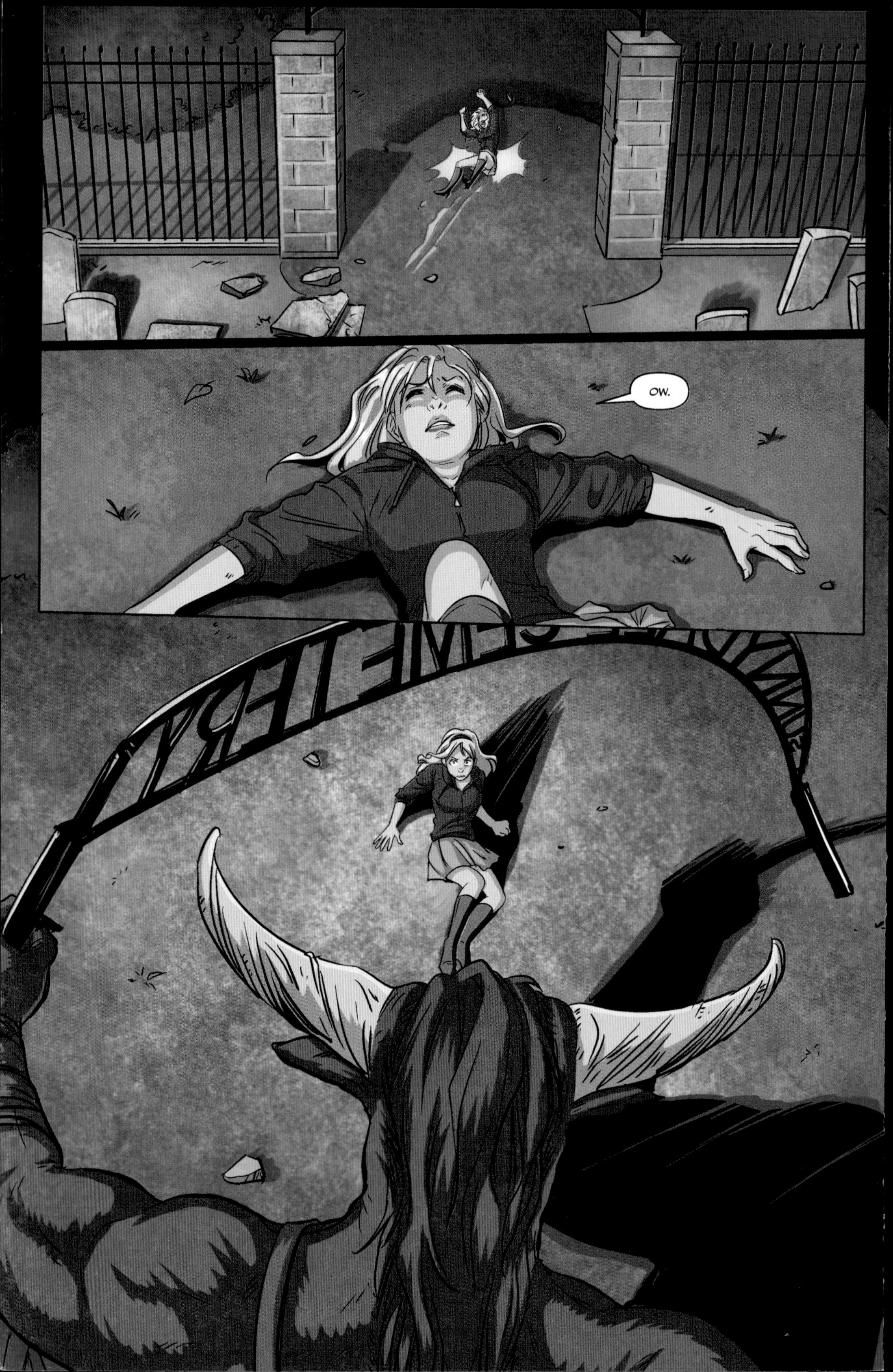
OW.

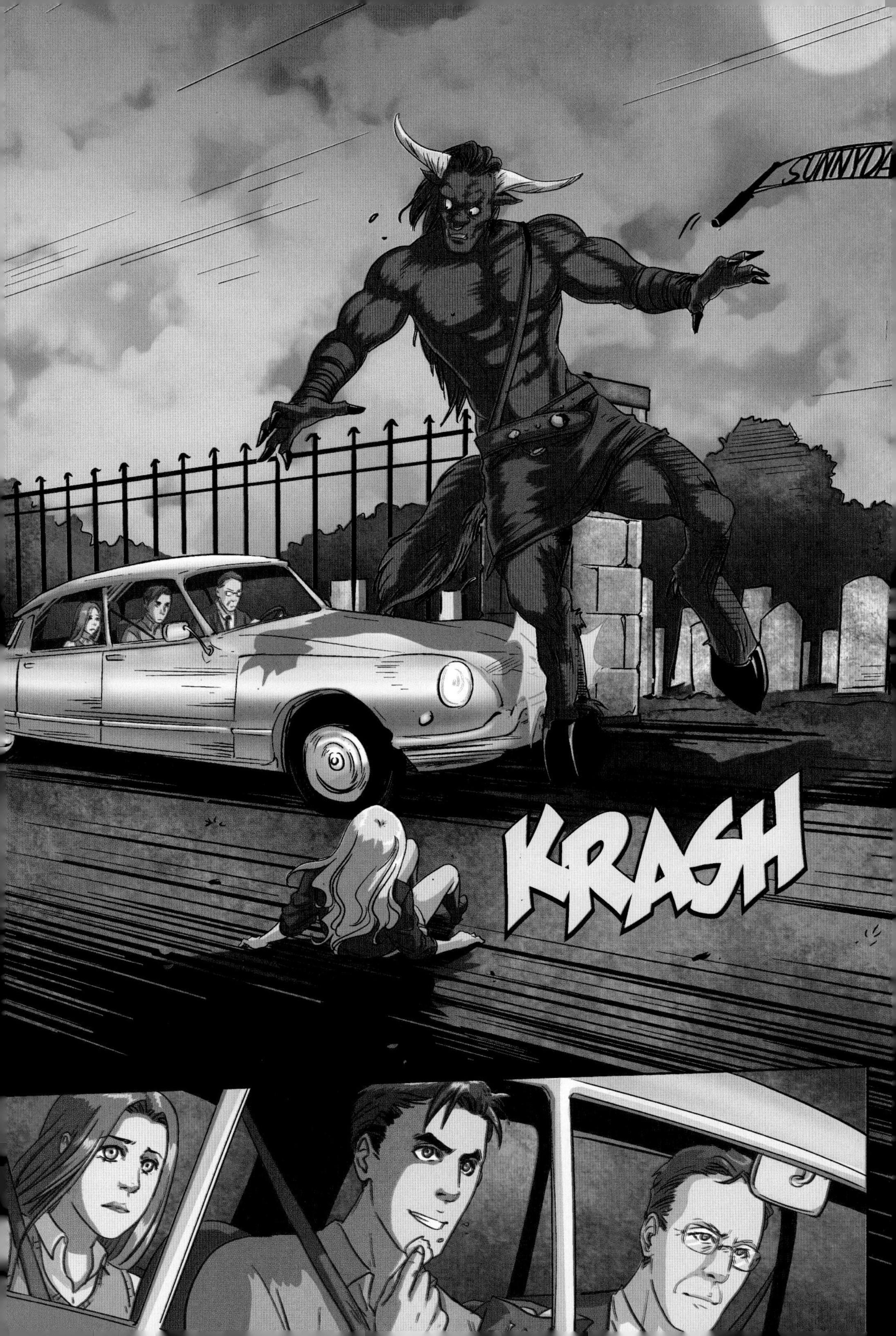
SUNNYDA
KRASH

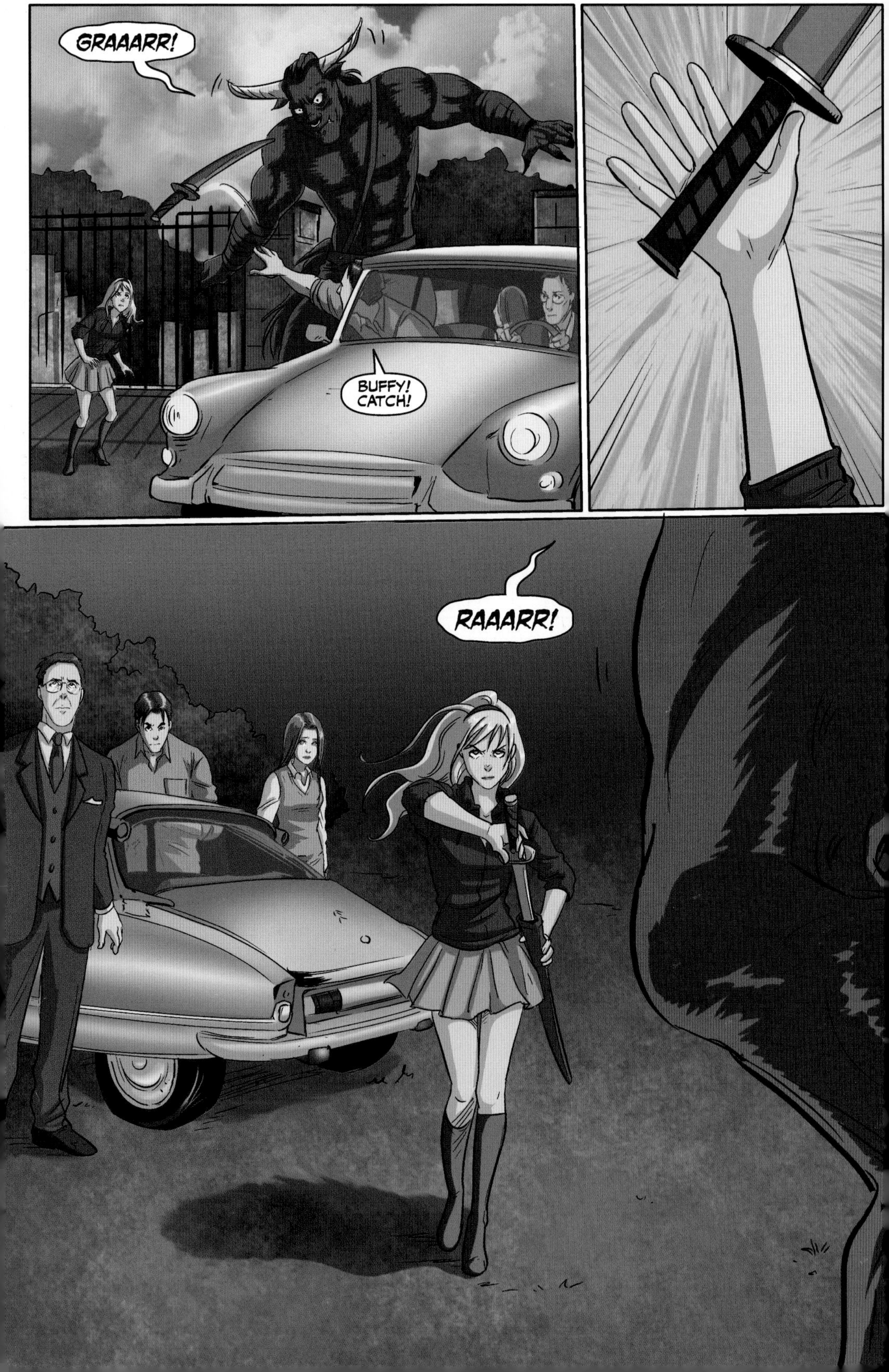
GRAAARR!
BUFFY! CATCH!
RAAARR!

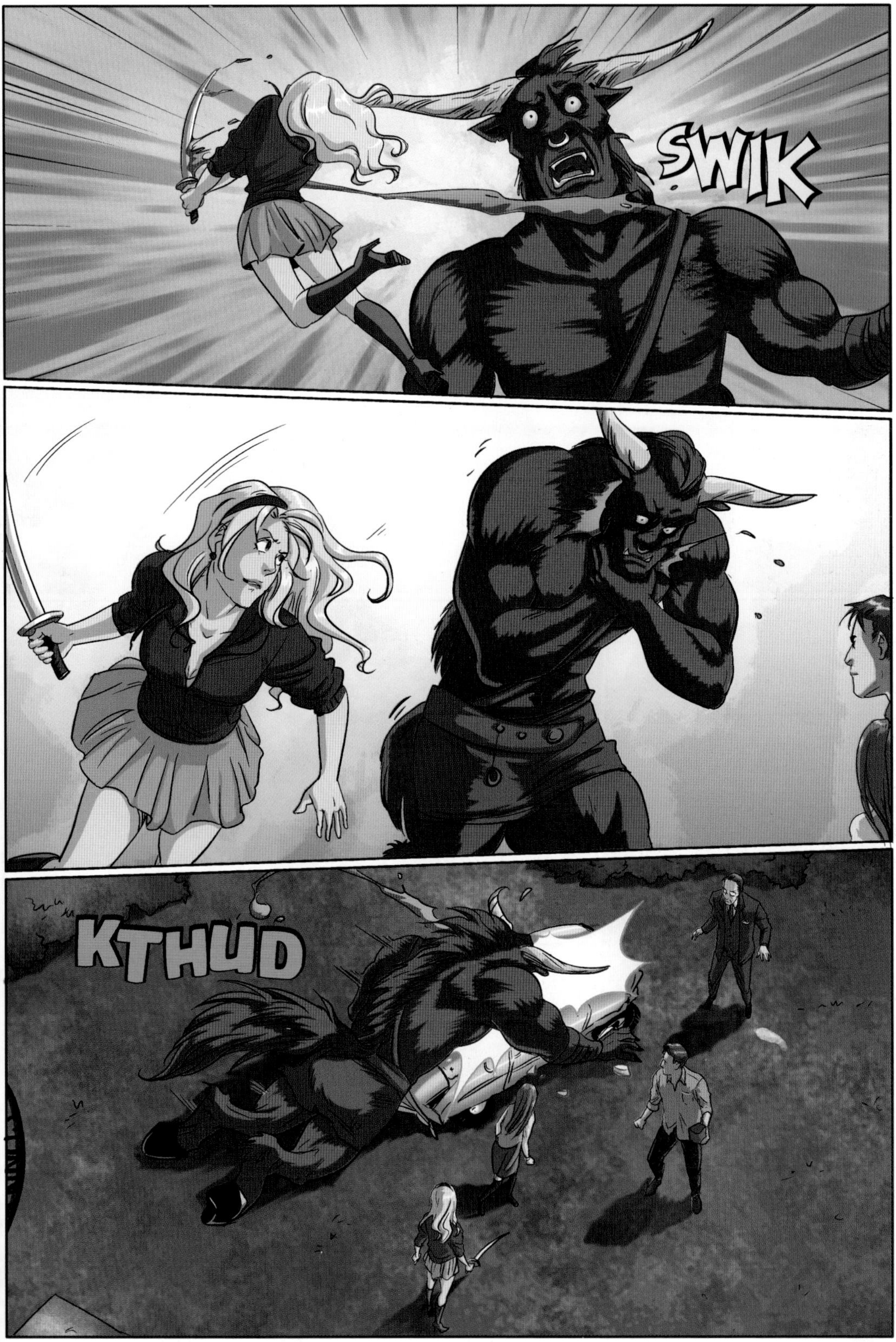
SWIK
KTHUD

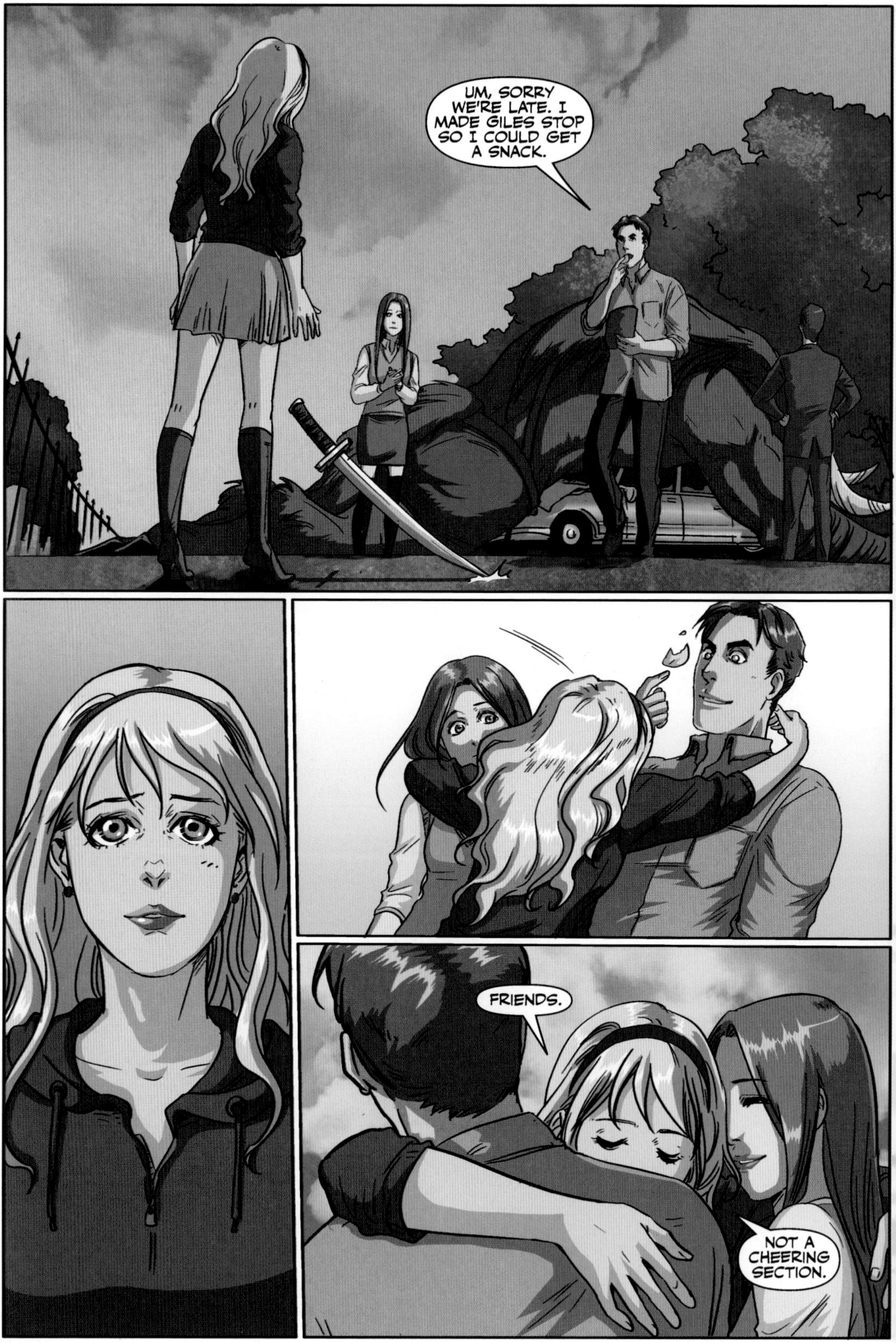
UM, SORRY WE'RE LATE. I MADE GILES STOP SO I COULD GET A SNACK.
FRIENDS.
NOT A CHEERING SECTION.

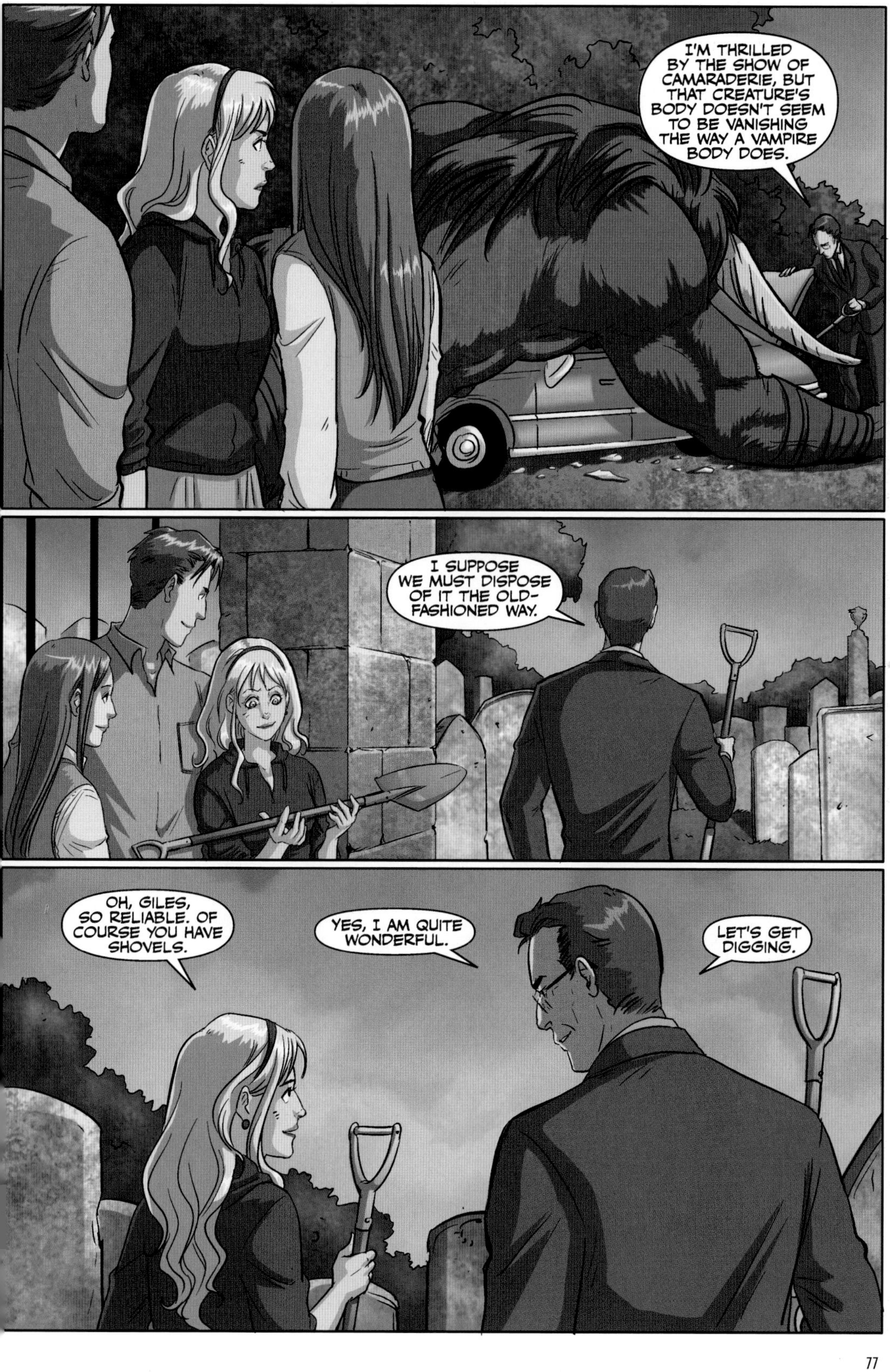
I'M THRILLED BY THE SHOW OF CAMARADERIE, BUT THAT CREATURE'S BODY DOESN'T SEEM TO BE VANISHING THE WAY A VAMPIRE BODY DOES.
I SUPPOSE WE MUST DISPOSE OF IT THE OLD-FASHIONED WAY.
OH, GILES, SO RELIABLE. OF COURSE YOU HAVE SHOVELS.
YES, I AM QUITE WONDERFUL.
LET'S GET DIGGING.

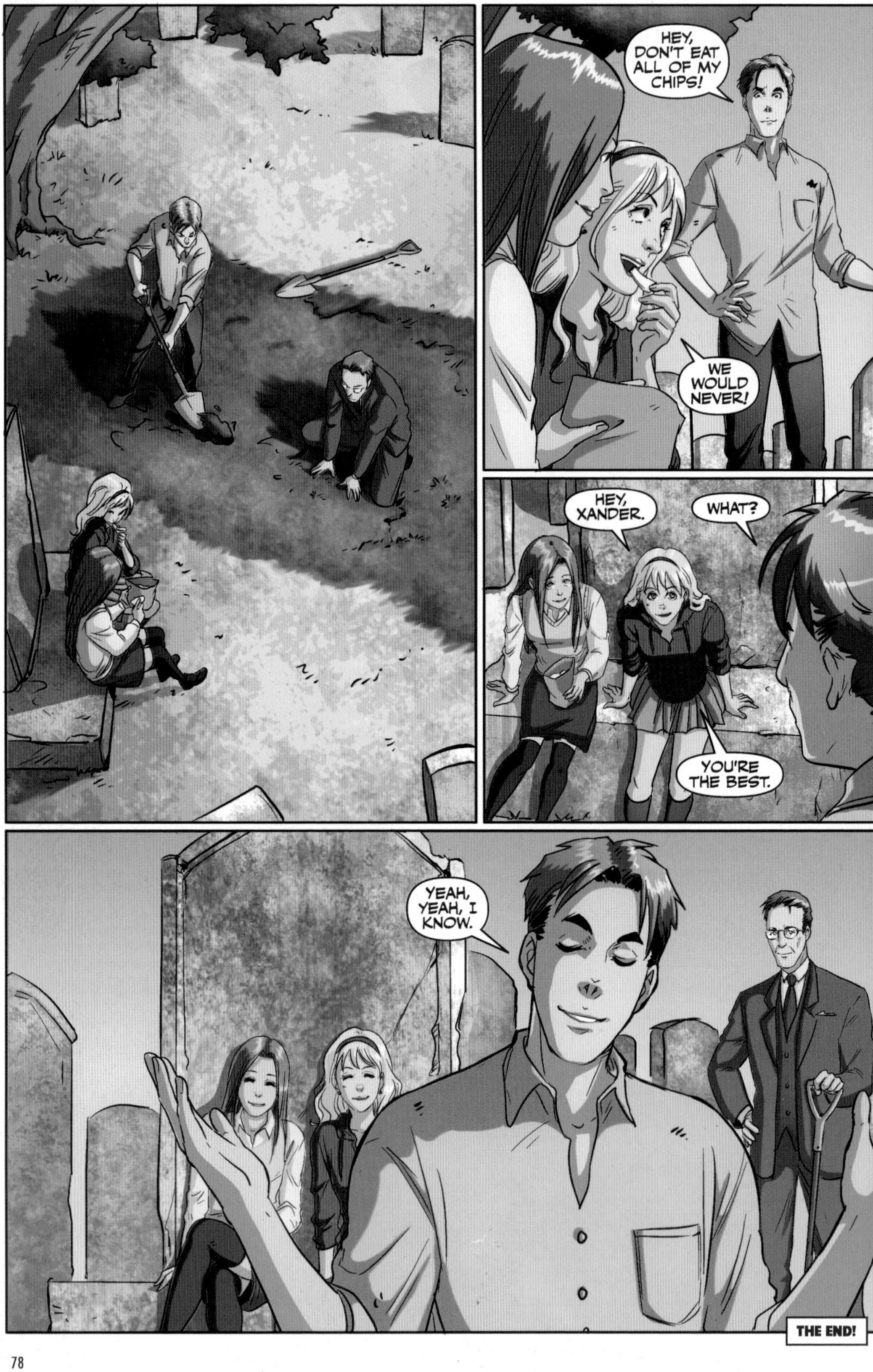
HEY, DON'T EAT ALL OF MY CHIPS!
WE WOULD NEVER!
HEY, XANDER.
WHAT?
YOU'RE THE BEST.
YEAH, YEAH, I KNOW.
THE END!

BUFFY THE VAMPIRE SLAYER SEASON 8

VOLUME 1: THE LONG WAY HOME
Joss Whedon and Georges Jeanty
ISBN 978-1-59307-822-5 | $15.99

VOLUME 2: NO FUTURE FOR YOU
Brian K. Vaughan, Georges Jeanty, and Joss Whedon
ISBN 978-1-59307-963-5 | $15.99

VOLUME 3: WOLVES AT THE GATE
Drew Goddard, Georges Jeanty, and Joss Whedon
ISBN 978-1-59582-165-2 | $15.99

VOLUME 4: TIME OF YOUR LIFE
Joss Whedon, Jeph Loeb, Georges Jeanty, and others
ISBN 978-1-59582-310-6 | $15.99

VOLUME 5: PREDATORS AND PREY
Joss Whedon, Jane Espenson, Georges Jeanty, Cliff Richards, and others
ISBN 978-1-59582-342-7 | $15.99

VOLUME 6: RETREAT
Joss Whedon, Jane Espenson, Georges Jeanty, Karl Moline, and others
ISBN 978-1-59582-415-8 | $15.99

VOLUME 7: TWILIGHT
Joss Whedon, Brad Meltzer, and Georges Jeanty
ISBN 978-1-59582-558-2 | $16.99

VOLUME 8: LAST GLEAMING
Joss Whedon, Scott Allie, and Georges Jeanty
ISBN 978-1-59582-610-7 | $16.99

BUFFY THE VAMPIRE SLAYER SEASON 8 LIBRARY EDITION

VOLUME 1 ISBN 978-1-59582-888-0 | $29.99
VOLUME 2 ISBN 978-1-59582-935-1 | $29.99
VOLUME 3 ISBN 978-1-59582-978-8 | $29.99
VOLUME 4 ISBN 978-1-61655-127-8 | $29.99

BUFFY THE VAMPIRE SLAYER SEASON 9

VOLUME 1: FREEFALL
Joss Whedon, Andrew Chambliss, Georges Jeanty, and others
ISBN 978-1-59582-922-1 | $17.99

VOLUME 2: ON YOUR OWN
Andrew Chambliss, Scott Allie, Georges Jeanty, and others
ISBN 978-1-59582-990-0 | $17.99

VOLUME 3: GUARDED
Joss Whedon, Jane Espenson, Drew Z. Greenberg, Georges Jeanty, and others
ISBN 978-1-61655-099-8 | $17.99

VOLUME 4: WELCOME TO THE TEAM
Andrew Chambliss, Georges Jeanty, Karl Moline, and others
ISBN 978-1-61655-166-7 | $17.99

VOLUME 5: THE CORE
Andrew Chambliss, Georges Jeanty, and others
ISBN 978-1-61655-254-1 | $17.99

BUFFY THE VAMPIRE SLAYER SEASON 9 LIBRARY EDITION

VOLUME 1 ISBN 978-1-61655-715-7 | $29.99
VOLUME 2 ISBN 978-1-61655-716-4 | $29.99
VOLUME 3 ISBN 978-1-61655-717-1 | $29.99

BUFFY THE VAMPIRE SLAYER SEASON 10

VOLUME 1: NEW RULES
Christos Gage, Rebekah Isaacs, Nicholas Brendon, and others
ISBN 978-1-61655-490-3 | $18.99

VOLUME 2: I WISH
Christos Gage, Rebekah Isaacs, Nicholas Brendon, and others
ISBN 978-1-61655-600-6 | $18.99

VOLUME 3: LOVE DARES YOU
Christos Gage, Rebekah Isaacs, Nicholas Brendon, and Megan Levens
ISBN 978-1-61655-758-4 | $18.99

VOLUME 4: OLD DEMONS
Christos Gage and Rebekah Isaacs
ISBN 978-1-61655-802-4 | $18.99

ANGEL & FAITH SEASON 9

VOLUME 1: LIVE THROUGH THIS
Christos Gage, Rebekah Isaacs, and Phil Noto
ISBN 978-1-59582-887-3 | $17.99

VOLUME 2: DADDY ISSUES
Christos Gage, Rebekah Isaacs, and Chris Samnee
ISBN 978-1-59582-960-3 | $17.99

VOLUME 3: FAMILY REUNION
Christos Gage, Rebekah Isaacs, Lee Garbett, and David Lapham
ISBN 978-1-61655-079-0 | $17.99

VOLUME 4: DEATH AND CONSEQUENCES
Christos Gage and Rebekah Isaacs
ISBN 978-1-61655-165-0 | $17.99

VOLUME 5: WHAT YOU WANT, NOT WHAT YOU NEED
Christos Gage and Rebekah Isaacs
ISBN 978-1-61655-253-4 | $17.99

ANGEL & FAITH SEASON 9 LIBRARY EDITION

VOLUME 1 ISBN 978-1-61655-712-6 | $29.99
VOLUME 2 ISBN 978-1-61655-713-3 | $29.99
VOLUME 3 ISBN 978-1-61655-714-0 | $29.99

ANGEL & FAITH SEASON 10

VOLUME 1: WHERE THE RIVER MEETS THE SEA
Victor Gischler, Will Conrad, Derlis Santacruz, and others
ISBN 978-1-61655-503-0 | $18.99

VOLUME 2: LOST AND FOUND
Victor Gischler and Will Conrad
ISBN 978-1-61655-601-3 | $18.99

VOLUME 3: UNITED
Victor Gischler and Will Conrad
ISBN 978-1-61655-766-9 | $18.99

VOLUME 4: A LITTLE MORE THAN KIN
Victor Gischler, Cliff Richards, and Will Conrad
ISBN 978-1-61655-890-1 | $18.99

SPIKE

VOLUME 1: A DARK PLACE
Victor Gischler and Paul Lee
ISBN 978-1-61655-109-4 | $17.99

SPIKE: INTO THE LIGHT
James Marsters and Derlis Santacruz
ISBN 978-1-61655-421-7 | $14.99

WILLOW

VOLUME 1: WONDERLAND
Jeff Parker, Christos Gage, and Brian Ching
ISBN 978-1-61655-145-2 | $17.99

Buffy the vampire slayer

AVAILABLE AT YOUR LOCAL COMICS SHOP OR BOOKSTORE!
To find a comics shop in your area, call 1-888-266-4226. For more information or to order direct:
On the web: DarkHorse.com • E-mail: mailorder@darkhorse.com • Phone: 1-800-862-0052 Mon.–Fri. 9 AM to 5 PM Pacific Time

DARK HORSE BOOKS